Matthew Henry's *Commentary* abides
of the Scriptures. Many people from
Spurgeon to the modern reader have
experiential refreshment in its pages. B
Puritan roots. Allan Harman's biograp
of information about Matthew Henry. ..... we discover his godly
father, Philip Henry, his upbringing during times of persecution, and
his faithful pastoral ministry in Chester, England. This book will be
of great interest to historians, students of the Puritans, pastors, and
thousands of others who continue to benefit from Henry's *Commentary*.
Harman blessed us once with the publication of Henry's sermons on
the covenant of grace, and now he brings a double blessing!

Joel R. Beeke,
President, Puritan Reformed Theological Seminary
Grand Rapids, Michigan

Matthew Henry's *Commentary* has enriched Christians' understanding
of Scriptures for over 300 years. Recognizing Henry as 'one of the
most significant writers since the Reformation,' Allan Harman's
biography *Matthew Henry* recounts the life of this faithful pastor, while
also opening a window into the world of the 17th century English
Puritans, whose heir Henry was. Henry's life spent in service for God
and communion with Him is an example needed in the 21st century
church, and gratitude is owed to Allan Harman for introducing this
godly man to us.

Diana Severance
Author of *Feminine Threads* and Historian, Spring, Texas

To anyone who can read this brilliant biography without being
humbled, challenged, inspired and motivated to 'press on toward the
goal', I have only one thing to say – read it again. I am struggling to
think of any biography that has spoken so clearly to me and it would
be impossible for me to commend it too highly.

John Blanchard
Internationally known Christian preacher, teacher, apologist and author
Surrey, England

It is exactly 350 years since Matthew Henry was born. My edition
of his world-famous Commentary on the whole Bible extends to six

large volumes and was published 175 years ago. I have prized and read and quoted it for almost 60 years, but I knew little or nothing about Matthew Henry's life. Allan Harman has put the whole Christian world in his debt by researching and writing this excellent and fascinating biography of a man outstanding in scholarship, preaching, prayerfulness, godliness and faithful pastoring of the same church for twenty years. Here we learn of his home and of the great privilege of being a son of his pastor, mentor and model, Philip Henry ('He brought up his children in the fear of God, and with much tenderness', Matthew tells us). His life had many trials and sorrows personally, and he lived through a most difficult period of church history (his birth coincided with the year of the Great Ejection). But his was a life of extraordinary fruitfulness. I found the story enthralling and deeply encouraging, and I earnestly hope that the book will have the widest readership. I for one am heartily grateful to Allan Harman and Christian Focus for it.

Eric Alexander
formerly minister of St George's Tron Church, Glasgow, Scotland

This is a fascinating and well researched biography of one of the great fathers of expository preaching. It will refresh the spirit of all who read it. Encouragingly we find that many factors, including family joys and personal tragedies, shaped the character of the man behind the most enduringly useful Bible commentary.

John Benton
Managing editor, *Evangelicals Now*

Matthew Henry (1662-1714):

His Life and Influence

To Rebekah and Adam
with many greetings in
the Lord.

Allan M. Harman

ALLAN M. HARMAN

CHRISTIAN
FOCUS

Copyright © Allan Harman 2012

ISBN 978-1-84550-783-1

Published in 2012
by
Christian Focus Publications
Geanies House, Fearn, Ross-shire,
IV20 1TW, Scotland

www.christianfocus.com

Cover design by Daniel van Straaten

Printed by Bell and Bain, Glasgow

CONTENTS

MATTHEW HENRY
(R. Cooper)

That a holy, heavenly life, spent in the service of God and communion with him, is the most pleasant and comfortable life that any one can live in this world.

Matthew Henry, 1714

PREFACE

My acquaintance with the name of Matthew Henry goes back to childhood days as my father would sometimes mention it when preaching. Then in 1953 he passed on to me a small vellum covered volume of twenty-nine sermons in Matthew Henry's own handwriting that he had earlier been given by a fellow pastor. I finally deciphered these and they were published by Christian Focus in 2003 under the title *The Unpublished Sermons of Matthew Henry on the Covenant of Grace*.

Over the years I have collected information on Matthew Henry and this biography is the outcome of research into his life, achievements and influence. He was a remarkable pastor and writer, whose written ministry has far exceeded the impact of his spoken ministry during his lifetime.

Unfortunately, Matthew Henry's own diary no longer exists. His father's *Diaries and Letters*, edited by a descendant, Matthew Henry Lee, were published in 1882 (London: Kegan Paul, Trench & Co.). It contains a note that further particulars about his mother, Katharine, 'will be given of her in "Matthew Henry's Letters and Diaries", which are shortly to be published' (p. 386). That volume never appeared. We are, therefore, dependent on parts of the diary that are quoted in books, especially in the biographies by William Tong and J. B. Williams.

I thank my wife Mairi once more for all her help. She has willingly accepted my pursuit of matters relating to Matthew Henry, and the manuscript is better for her comments. Again, too, I thank my friend from school days, Bernard Secombe, whose eye for detail and felicitious phrasing is much appreciated. My gratitude also goes to John and Sarah Nicholls for reading the manuscript and commenting on it. I am indebted to Tanya Assender for assistance in preparation of the illustrations.

Allan M. Harman

CHAPTER I

The Puritan Environment

The year in which Matthew Henry was born was a momentous one for the religious history of England. In that year, 1662, over 2000 pastors were ejected from their parishes in the Church of England because they refused to conform to the requirements laid upon them by the Act of Uniformity. This meant that those pastors who were labelled as nonconformists, and who became Presbyterian, Baptist or Congregational, were deprived of opportunities to minister publicly, and nonconformist students were excluded from Oxford and Cambridge Universities. The fact that Matthew Henry's father, Philip Henry, was one of those ejected brought the religious issues of the day right into the family circle.

But the Great Ejection, as it was called, was only one of several important events in seventeenth-century England. It was marked by the overthrow of the monarchy and the Church of England, and then their subsequent re-establishment. The rift between Charles I and the Parliament became so great that two civil wars eventuated (1642-48), in which Royalists were pitted against Roundheads, the nickname for supporters of the Parliament. The Parliament's New Model Army was victorious and Charles I was executed in January 1649. Previously executed were Thomas Wentworth, Earl of Strafford, the Lord Lieutenant of Ireland (May 1641), and William Laud, the Archbishop of

Canterbury (January 1645). Episcopal rule in the church was set aside, and use of the Book of Common Prayer outlawed. The Westminster Assembly met from 1643 to 1658, and its greatest product, the Westminster Confession of Faith, was adopted in Scotland but not in England. The Savoy Conference was held in 1660 in an attempt to thrash out a compromise settlement that would allow many of Puritan persuasion to remain in the Church of England. That conference was unsuccessful.

However, the monarchy was re-established in 1660, and bishops, with seats in the House of Lords, regained power. Laws authorised repression of worship in which the Book of Common Prayer was not used, and many nonconformists were persecuted. But even greater change occurred in 1688. Charles II, who became King in 1660, had died in 1685 and was succeeded by his brother, James II. He was staunchly Roman Catholic, and when his second wife gave birth to a son, Protestant politicians in England moved and invited William of Orange to come and be king of England. Along with a Dutch army, he landed in Torbay, Devonshire, on 5 November 1688, and in the following year an Act of Parliament gave religious toleration to all Protestants, and the throne became and remained Protestant.

The seventeenth century was also noted as being within the Puritan period and very distinguished men taught and preached, including men like John Owen, William Perkins and William Gurnall. The Puritan period had come to a close by the time Richard Baxter died in 1692, though Matthew Henry and some of his associates carried the Puritan learning and vision over into the eighteenth century.

To define Puritanism and to delineate its commencement and end remain difficult.[1] Definition is difficult because the

---

1   For discussions on the meaning of the word 'Puritan', see Christopher Hill, *Society and Puritanism in Pre-Revolutionary England* (London: Secker and Warburg, 1958), chap. 1; Basil Hall, 'Puritanism: The Problem of Definition', *Studies in Church History*, vol. 2, ed. G. J. Cumming (London: Thomas Nelson, 1965), pp. 283-96; Randall C. Gleason and Kelly M. Kapic, eds., *The Devoted Life: An Invitation to the Puritan Classics* (Downers Grove: InterVarsity Press, 2004), pp. 15-37.

word 'puritan', first used in the 1560s in England, was a word of
abuse directed at a group of Christians. Shakespeare, in *Twelfth
Night* (c. 1599), portrayed them as people to be despised, for
example, when Maria says of Malvolio, 'Sir, sometimes he is
a kind of puritan', Sir Andrew replies, 'O, if I thought that, I'd
beat him like a dog'.[2] In regard to their way of life, the Puritans
were 'precise'. Richard Rogers of Wethersfield in Essex, an
influential Puritan figure, was once told by a gentleman: 'Mr
Rogers, I like you and your company very well, only you are *too
precise.*' 'Oh, sir', replied Rogers, 'I serve a precise God.' That was
a fitting reply, for clearly the Puritans had a deep commitment
to the Bible as God's revealed will and they wished to conform
their personal lives and the life of the church to God's demands
expressed in it. The very first sentence in William Ames's *Marrow
of Sacred Divinity* is: 'Divinity is the doctrine of living to God'.[3]

Let J. I. Packer give a summary of what constituted Puritanism:

> Puritanism ... was a total view of Christianity, Bible-based,
> church-centred, God-honouring, literate, orthodox, pastoral,
> and Reformational, that saw personal, domestic, professional,
> political, churchly, and economic existence as aspects of
> a single whole, and that called on everybody to order every
> department and every relationship of their life according
> to the Word of God, so that all would be sanctified and
> become 'holiness to the Lord'. Puritanism's spearhead activity
> was pastoral evangelism and nurture through preaching,
> catechising, and counselling (which Puritans themselves
> called casuistry), and Puritan teaching harped constantly on
> the themes of self-knowledge, self-humbling, and repentance;
> faith in, and love for, Jesus Christ the Saviour; the necessity
> of regeneration, and of sanctification (holy living, by God's

---

2   *Twelfth Night*, II.iii.128-154.

3   William Ames, *Marrow of Sacred Divinity* (London: Henry Overton, 1642), p. 1.
    Ames (or the Latinised form of his name and by which he was widely known,
    Amesius) was highly influential on Reformed theology, and his *Marrow* was still
    being used in the training of Free Church students in Scotland until late in the
    nineteenth century.

power) as proof of it; the need for conscientious conformity to all God's law, and for a disciplined use of the means of grace; and the blessedness of the assurance and joy from the Holy Spirit that all faithful believers under ordinary circumstances may know. Puritans saw themselves as God's pilgrims, travelling home; God's warriors, battling against the world, the flesh and the devil; and God's servants, under order to do all the good they could as they went along.[4]

Politically the Puritan pastors were not a unified group. Some, probably the majority, were avowedly Republicans, serving as chaplains in the army of Oliver Cromwell, the Protector of England, and even, like John Howe, as the Protector's domestic chaplain. Their republicanism did not mean that they necessarily approved of the execution of Charles I. Richard Baxter noted in his autobiography that he abhorred it, and did everything in his power to prevent it. However, other Puritans were Royalists, who had no real love for Cromwell, and were very suspicious of his motives. Many others would probably have remained Royalists were it not for the ungodliness of so many in that group.

While having close doctrinal unity, the Puritans differed on many other questions, especially concerning the interaction of faith and politics, as well as the nature of the church. This fragmentation hindered their overall influence on English life. Richard Baxter and others said 'that if all the Presbyterians had been like Mr Stephen Marshall, and all the Independents like Mr Jeremiah Burroughs, and all the Episcopal men like Archbishop Ussher, the breaches of the church would soon have been healed'.[5]

---

4   J. I. Packer, *Collected Shorter Writings of J. I. Packer: Honouring the People of God*, vol. 4 (Carlisle: Paternoster Press, 1999), pp. 24-5. The same volume contains another similar summary of Puritanism on p. 265.

5   Matthew Henry, *The Life of the Rev. Philip Henry, A.M. with Funeral Sermons for Mr and Mrs Henry* (first published 1828; reprinted Edinburgh: Banner of Truth Trust, 1974), p. 6. This biography was first published in 1698, and the reprint is the edition put out by J. B. Williams in 1825. It is cited hereafter as *The Life of the Rev. Philip Henry*.

The Puritans have not been without their defenders, and in the nineteenth century none defended them so strongly as J. C. Ryle, Bishop of Liverpool (1880-1900). Writing almost 130 years ago, his words still stand true. He was writing on Richard Baxter, but in so doing he was taking a far more comprehensive view and did so as an Anglican bishop, not a nonconformist defending the Puritans. This is how he described them:

> Let us settle it down in our minds that for sound doctrine, spirituality and learning combined, the Puritans stand at the head of English divines. With all their faults, weaknesses, and defects, they alone kept the lamp of pure, Evangelical religion burning in this country in the times of the Stuarts,—they alone prevented Laud's Popish inclinations carrying England back into the arms of Rome. It was they who fought the battle of religious freedom, of which we are reaping such fruits. It was they who crushed the wretched spirit of inquisitorial persecution which misguided High Churchmen tried to introduce into this land. Let us give them the honour they deserve. Let us suffer no man to speak lightly of them in our presence. Let us remember our obligations to them, reverence their memory, stand up boldly for their reputation, and never be afraid to plead their cause. It is the cause of pure, Evangelical religion. It is the cause of an open Bible and liberty to meet, and read, and pray together. It is the cause of liberty of conscience. All these are bound up with Baxter and the Puritans. Let us remember this, and give them their due.[6]

As already noted, it is hard to pinpoint the exact time the Puritan period began, and also when it finished. Certainly its origins go back as far as William Tyndale, and perhaps the year 1526, when his New Testament in English reached England, can be regarded as the starting point, though the term 'puritan' was not used until 1563. In that year Stow made a reference to 'many congregations of Anabaptysts in London who

---

6   J. C. Ryle, *Facts and Men, being pages from English Church History, Some Biographical and Some Historical between 1553 and 1683, with a Preface for the Times* (London: William Hunt and Co., 1882), pp. 323-4.

cawlyd themselves Puritans or unspotted Lambs of the Lord'.[7] With the progress of the Reformation movement in England, Queen Elizabeth I established the Elizabethan Compromise, which did not contain sufficient for those of the Reformed party, who soon would be called 'Puritans'. 'Thus it began', to use Peter Lewis' words, 'under Elizabeth I who suspected it, grew under James I who feared it, increased in power under Charles I and his Archbishop, William Laud, who despised it, gained a brief but august ascendency under Cromwell who honoured it, and ended under Charles II and his bishops who hated it'.[8]

Clearly the term 'puritan' was strictly a reference to those within the Anglican Church who 'desired some modifications in Church government and worship'.[9] If the strict usage is followed, this would put the end of the Puritan era at about the start of the Civil War in 1642. But the word 'Puritan' has also obtained a wider meaning and so some flexibility in usage, both as to the beginning of the period and its end, is desirable. To date the end of the Puritan period in the 1640s is probably putting the close of the era a little too early. Certainly the Puritan era had waned considerably by the time William of Orange was proclaimed King in 1688 (the so-called 'Glorious Revolution'), as the nonconformists from that point onwards had the right to preach and to establish independent churches. The terminology had also changed in that instead of 'Puritan' there is reference to Presbyterians, Independents, Baptists, and Quakers. The death of Richard Baxter in 1691 marked the end of a great era of biblical scholarship, though some others lived into the next century. John Howe, for example, lived until 1705. Matthew Henry

---

7   Quoted in *The Century Dictionary* (London: Century Co., 1914), vol. VII under the word 'Puritan'.

8   Peter Lewis, *The Genius of Puritanism* (Haywards Heath: Carey Publications, 1975), p. 14.

9   B. Hall, 'Puritanism: The Problem of Definition', p. 289.

carried on that tradition as a second-generation scholar until his death in 1714, and while he did not study personally under the great scholars whose instruction so influenced his father, yet his ministry of preaching and writing continued the Puritan influence into the eighteenth century.

In a way it does not matter greatly where the exact chronological boundaries are placed in regard to the Puritans. What does matter is that the period when they were so dominant in English life exhibits Christianity as taking hold of the total life experience of many people, and that world-and-life view (to use a much more modern phrase) in turn influenced many in the British Isles, the Netherlands, and in the American colonies. While no similar period in church history can be called Puritan in the same sense, yet individuals have exhibited many of the same characteristics, including Charles Haddon Spurgeon (1834-1892), and Martyn Lloyd-Jones (1899-1981), whom J. I. Packer calls 'a kind of Puritan'.[10]

---

10   J. I. Packer, *Honouring the People of God: Collected Shorter Writings of J. I. Packer*, vol. 4, p. 61.

CHAPTER 2

The Family Background

Matthew Henry came from a family and home that were deeply imbued with Puritan beliefs. His father Philip was born in Whitehall, London, in 1631 of a Welsh father and an English mother, Magdalen Rochdale. Philip's father, John Henry, though from a very humble background, rose to become 'gentleman' to the Earl of Pembroke, and when Pembroke became Lord Chamberlain, John Henry served the king, Charles I. His wife was from a noble family, though clearly she had come to a strong personal faith in Christ, and she endeavoured to teach her children the ways of the Lord. Having only one son, she committed him to the service of God in the work of the ministry.

Philip Henry had his early schooling near the family home in inner London, first of all at a Latin school connected with St Martin's Church, and afterwards at Battersea. When he was twelve years old he became a pupil at the Westminster School, and obtained a thorough classical education in Greek and Latin. There, under Dr Richard Busby, he obtained an education that stood him in good stead for the rest of his life. Sometime after Philip Henry was ejected from his living at Worthenbury in Flintshire in 1662, he met up with his former teacher who asked him, 'Prithee, Child, what made thee a nonconformist?'

The answer was: 'Truly, Sir, you made me one, for you taught me those things that hindered me from conforming.' When Philip Henry heard in 1695 (one year before his own death) that Dr Busby had died after nearly 58 years of teaching at the Westminster School, he wrote: 'I believe I have as much reason to bless God for him, as any scholar that ever he had', he having been so used of God in beginning the work of grace in him.[1] It was during this time that his mother sought permission from his teacher for him to attend the daily morning lectures by members of the Westminster Assembly of Divines (from six o'clock to eight o'clock). At this time spiritual issues gripped him, and he was clearly 'begotten again to a living hope' (1 Pet. 1:3). On Sundays he sat under the ministry of Rev. Stephen Marshall in the mornings at New Chapel, while in the afternoons he attended St Margaret's, Westminster, which was the family's parish church. From about the age of eleven or twelve, Philip Henry took notes of the sermons he heard, and afterwards transcribed them in a full text.

Philip Henry was chosen as a King's scholar at Oxford, entering Christ Church as a commoner in December 1647. His godfather, the Earl of Pembroke, gave him ten pounds with which to buy a gown, and to pay his fees. This gift, wrote Philip Henry in his diary, was 'a seasonable mercy, in regard to some straits whereinto God in His Providence had brought my deare Father'.[2] In March, 1648, he was admitted as a student of Christ Church, by the Sub-Dean, Dr Henry Hammond, who was also a godchild of the Earl of Pembroke. Because of this he called Philip Henry his godbrother!

---

1   H. D. Roberts, *Matthew Henry and His Chapel 1662-1900* (Liverpool: The Liverpool Booksellers Company, 1900), pp. 10-11. This book is hereafter cited as *Matthew Henry and His Chapel*.

2   M. H. Lee, ed., *Diaries and Letters of Philip Henry, M.A. of Broad Oak, Flintshire A.D. 1631-1696* (London: Kegan Paul, Trench & Co., 1882), p. 11. This book is hereafter cited as *Diaries and Letters of Philip Henry*.

At that time the universities were under the power of the Parliament, but no change was made at Oxford until a group representing the Parliament came in April 1647. Among this group was the Earl of Pembroke. All staff and students were faced with a single question: 'Will you submit to the power of the Parliament in this present visitation?' The response was to be given in writing, and depending on the answer they either stayed at the university or they were removed. When faced with the question Philip Henry answered: 'I submit to the power of the Parliament in the present visitation, as far as I may with a safe conscience, and without perjury.' While it was not an absolutely direct answer, yet it seemed to satisfy, and by the grace of his godfather he was continued as a student.

Students were placed under particular masters, and his tutor, Mr Underwood, was one of those removed because they would not acknowledge the power of the Parliament. Philip Henry was put into the care of Mr William Finmore, who did not have the ability of the previous tutor. Fortunately, an older student from Westminster, Richard Bryan, took an interest in Philip Henry, sharing his room with him and overseeing his studies for the rest of his time at Oxford. Daily discussions were held in term time, along with weekly recitations and declamations (set speeches in public), at which he shone.

His contemporaries at Oxford were of two kinds. First, there were 'the new stamp' that came in after the visitation, 'pious souls, but of smal abilityes comparatively for learning'. On the other hand, there 'were those of the old spirit and way, that were for Bishops and Common-prayer'. While these were the better scholars, Philip Henry recognised later that though that was so, they were not better men, and his association with them almost ruined him.[3]

---

3 This information is not in the diary of Philip Henry as published by Matthew Henry Lee, but it appears in Matthew Henry's life of his father (*The Life of the Rev. Philip Henry*, p. 17), and also quoted by Roberts, *Matthew Henry and His Chapel,* p. 8. Either the omission was deliberate by M. H. Lee, or the diary was extant in two forms.

Clearly all was not well with him in the early part of his time at Oxford. One temptation was that he did not have to study too hard to keep up with his fellow students, for his schooling had been superior to that of many others. Also, he was young and found it easy to turn from study, and consequently spent a lot of time at recreations such as bowling. He also went, especially on winter mornings, to a tavern to drink metheglin, a Welsh alcoholic liquor made from fermented honey. Looking back on that time he wrote: 'For ever praised be the riches of God's free grace, that he was pleased still to keep his hold of me; and not to let me alone when I was running from him, but set his hand again the second time, as the expression is, Isa. 11:11, to snatch me as a brand out of the fire.'[4] The change that came over him he regarded as a kind of second conversion, and from then on he was truly committed to Christ. When he later returned to Oxford on a visit, he would think about this early period of his studies and he said that 'a tear dropt over my University sins'.[5]

At the end of 1648 Philip Henry got permission to go to London to see his father. He was present in the crowd when Charles I was beheaded on 30 January 1649. In his own words, he:

> stood amongst the crowd in the street, before Whitehall gate, where the scaffold was erected, and saw what was done, but was not so near as to hear any thing. The Blow I saw given, & can truly say with a sad heart; at the instant whereof, I remember wel, there was such a Grone by the Thousands then present, as I never heard before & desire I may never hear again.[6]

Ever afterwards he testified his profound abhorrence of that deed, though acknowledging that not one in ten among the people approved of it, nor that the Parliament could be blamed, for most of the Parliamentarians were in prison. For

---

4   Matthew Henry, *The Life of the Rev. Philip Henry*, p. 17.

5   Roberts, *Matthew Henry and His Chapel*, p. 11.

6   Lee, *Diaries and Letters of Philip Henry*, p. 12.

some years he kept a day of humiliation on the anniversary of the execution, praying that God would 'deliver the nation from blood-guiltiness'. Later, however, he realised there was no instruction in Scripture to keep annual remembrance of particular sins such as this one, and so he dropped the practice.

In 1651 he took his Bachelor of Arts degree, and in his diary he thanked God for friends who had helped him with his expenses. Also, he recorded his gratitude that, in addition to his studies, he had the opportunity to grow in the Christian faith. Gatherings for discussions and prayer were held, and these seem to have been directed especially towards preparation for service in God's church. Moreover, every Lord's Day afternoon a university sermon was preached, and in his time Dr John Owen and Dr Thomas Goodwin took this alternately. Again, he followed the practice of writing out the sermons, not at the time of delivery, but afterwards as he reflected on what he had heard. During the Commonwealth period (1649-1660) Oxford enjoyed a time of spiritual life that resembled that of Cambridge a little earlier. Matthew Henry recalled hearing his father speak of:

> what great helps and advantages he had then in the University, not only for learning, but for religion and piety. Serious godliness was in reputation, and besides the publick opportunities they had, there were many of the scholars that used to meet together for prayer, and Christian conference, to the great confirming of one another's hearts in the fear and love of God, and the preparing of them for the service of the church in their generation.[7]

In December of the following year (1652) he took his Master of Arts degree, and as his reputation as a scholar had grown by this time he was called upon out of all the masters to give the Latin oration at vespers on philosophy questions. It was in this way that Dr John Owen, the Vice-Chancellor, became aware of his gifts and commended him highly.

---

7   Matthew Henry, *The Life of the Rev. Philip Henry*, p. 19.

Prior to leaving Oxford in 1653, Philip Henry preached his first sermon at South Hinksey in Oxford. The text he chose was John 8:34: 'Whosoever committeth sin is the servant of sin.' In his diary he recorded his prayer: 'The Lord make use of me as an instrument of his glory, and his church's good, in this high and holy calling.'[8]

On the recommendation of a fellow student, Philip Henry took up a tutor's position in the home of Judge and Lady Puleston in Worthenbury in Flintshire. It was Lady Puleston who had the greater spiritual interest. There was some reluctance on his part to accept such an appointment in the country as he was looking for an academic position in Oxford. However, Henry agreed to take the position for six months, overseeing the education of the sons in the family, and preaching once on the Lord's Day. He did not wish to preach twice, seeing that he was newly entering into this work, and went on the condition that someone else would preach at the second service. He quickly settled into life at the Pulestons' property, 'Emral', and when the second preacher failed to arrive one Sunday he took the second service, and thereafter carried on with the two services. The effectiveness of his work is attested by a letter that Lady Puleston sent him at the end of this six-month period. In it she wrote:

> This I am sure, that having wanted hitherto a good ministry of the word among us, I have oft by prayer and some tears, about five years besought God for such a one as yourself; which, having obtained, I cannot yet despair, seeing he hath given us the good means, but he may also give us the good end. And this I find, that your audience is increased three to one in the parish, though in winter more than formerly in summer; and five for one out of the other places.... I think I can name four or five in the parish, that of formal Christians are becoming or become real.... It is a good sign that most are loath to part with you; and you have done more good in this half year, than I have discerned these eighteen years.[9]

---

8   Ibid., p. 20.

9   Ibid., p. 26.

Despite the encouragement of knowing that his work had been blessed at 'Emral', Henry returned to Oxford in the spring of 1654, but Lady Puleston followed him there with her five sons, two of whom she left in his care at the university. In the summer he went to London to visit his relatives, and while there he received in October a letter from Judge Puleston. In it, the Judge expressed his wish, and that of the parishioners at Worthenbury, that he would return to become their minister. With generous provision by himself, he promised that Henry would receive £100 per annum 'until such times as the said Philip Henry shall be promoted or preferred to some other spiritual or ecclesiastical living or preferment'.[10] And so he acquiesced and continued some years with the Puleston family, at first continuing to live with them and then latterly in the house that Judge Puleston had erected for him. The lease granted him (dated 6 March 1657) stated that he could use the house for a period of sixty years, providing he continued as minister at Worthenbury!

In 1657 Philip Henry was nominated and presented as minister of the church at Worthenbury. This meant that he could now be ordained. The nearest presbytery as set up by the Parliament in 1647 comprised ministers at Prees, Wem, Newport, Ightfield and Hanmer, and it ordained sixty-three ministers in the space of twelve years. While Philip Henry wanted his ordination to be performed in the presence of his people at Worthenbury, the presbytery would not yield to what was a proposed new custom. Hence he was ordained at Prees on 16 September 1657. His examination followed the normal Presbyterian pattern: examinations in Greek and Hebrew, logic and philosophy, and divinity. He also had to write a thesis in Latin on the subject, 'An Providentia Divina extendat se ad omnia?' ('Does divine providence extend to everything?'). He also had to present a confession of his faith, which was virtually a summary of Christian doctrine.

---

10 Ibid., p. 27.

A large crowd assembled for the ordination, notification having been given that if 'any one could produce any just exceptions against the doctrine or life of the said Mr Henry, or any sufficient reason why he might not be ordained, they should certify the same to the classis, or the scribe, and it should be heard and considered'. Rev. Thomas Porter presided and Rev. Andrew Parson preached on 1 Timothy 1:12; and then these ministers along with Revs Aylmar Houghton, John Malden and Richard Steel[11] laid hands on him during prayer, and he was duly ordained to the office of the ministry. Another five ordinations followed at the same classis meeting.[12]

Henry continued the ministry that he had already been carrying out for some time previous to his ordination. Soon after, he administered the Lord's Supper for the first time. The parish consisted of forty-one communicants, and despite blessing on his ministry the total number never doubled during his time. The parish was small, and most of the people were poor tenant farmers. He preached through the Scripture in order, and in a manuscript surviving among his papers were some words by Rev. Thomas Porter on preaching that he sought to emulate:

Let your preaching be plain. Painted glass is most curious; plain glass is most perspicuous. Be a good crucifix to your people. Preach a crucified Saviour in a crucified style. Paul taught so plainly, that the Corinthians thought him a dunce. Let your matter be substantial; wholesome food; God and Christ, and the gospel, faith, repentance, regeneration. Aim purely at God's glory and the salvation of souls. Study, as if there were no Christ; preach, as if there had been no study. Preach plainly, yet with novelty; preach powerfully, as Micah; — as Paul, in intension of spirit, not extension of voice. To this end get your sermons into your own souls. It is best, from the heart, to the heart. Preach prudentially,—as stewards, to

---

11   Rev. Richard Steel lived long enough to take part in the ordination of Philip Henry's son Matthew on 9 May 1687, almost thirty years later.

12   Matthew Henry, *The Life of the Rev. Philip Henry*, p. 36.

give each their portion. Get your sermons memoriter [from memory]. How can you expect your people should remember, and repeat, if you read? Yet use caution. Our memories are not of brass,—they are cracked, in all, by the fall. Beware of giving occasion to say,— I may stay at home in the afternoon; I shall hear only the same song.[13]

Philip Henry kept detailed notes of his sermons, though he often included hints that were enlarged upon in delivery. He advised other preachers not to tie themselves down too closely to their notes, but, if the preparation had been carefully done, to allow for liberty of expression when preaching.

Pastoral visitation was carried out, monthly conferences held for the Christians, the sick and bereaved were ministered to, and he was often called upon to preach at weekday meetings in neighbouring parishes. So heavy were his ministrations that someone suggested to him that he ease up, for he was like a man lighting his whole pound of candles at the one time! He set aside a tenth of his salary for the poor and took a special interest in the education of needy families. One of his sayings in reference to giving was: 'He is no fool who parts with that which he cannot keep, when he is sure to be recompensed with that which he cannot lose.'

During the earlier part of his ministry a sister kept house for him. After some time he became friendly with Katharine Matthews, the only child of a wealthy couple who lived at Broad Oak, a farm situated in the township of Iscoyd in Flintshire.[14] Katharine's father was opposed to his daughter and heir contemplating marriage with Philip Henry. Some of her friends were also opposed. They claimed that while Mr Henry was a gentleman, a scholar and an excellent preacher, yet they did

---

13   Ibid., p. 25, fn.

14   The old farmhouse at Broad Oak was demolished about 1746 for an agent acting for Matthew Henry's son, Philip Henry Warburton. The timber from it was sufficient to build four other houses. See Lee, *Diaries and Letters of Philip Henry*, pp. 124-5.

not know where he came from. 'True,' replied Katharine, 'but I know where he is going, and I should like to go with him.' Ultimately true love prevailed and the couple were married on 26 April 1660. It was a marriage that was to last for just over forty-six years and to produce six children – John, Matthew, Sarah, Katharine, Eleanor and Ann. John died of measles when he was six, but the others were spared to grow to adulthood.

Matthew, the second child and second son of the family, was born on 18 October 1662. The year or two before and the period after his birth were tumultuous ones for the whole family. In September 1660 Philip Henry, along with Rev. Richard Fogg and Rev. Richard Steel, were taken to the Flint Assizes (the local court) because they were not using the Book of Common Prayer in their regular services. This was done in spite of the fact that such reading was not yet demanded by legislation. Despite that, Steel and Henry were again, within a few months, brought before the court. In his diary Philip Henry wrote: 'Be merciful to me, O God, for man would swallow me up! The Lord show me what he would have me to do, for I am afraid of nothing but sin'.[15]

Late in 1660 he took the oath of allegiance, and went out of his way to try to show that he was accommodating to the changed political and ecclesiastical situation. Along with some other ministers he preached on Christmas Day, acknowledging that there were divinely ordained feasts and also ecclesiastical feasts such as the Jewish ones of 'Purim' and 'Dedication' [of the Temple], now called 'Hanukkah'. He took as his Christmas text: 'For this purpose the Son of God was manifested, that he might destroy the works of the devil' (1 John 3:8).

But Philip Henry did not go far enough and his annuity of £100 was withheld because he did not read from the Book of

---

15   Matthew Henry, *The Life of the Rev. Philip Henry*, p. 89. The last phrase appears to be a quotation from Chrysostom (AD 345-407), who having offended the Empress Eudoxia, was sent a threatening message. He replied: *Nil nisi peccatum timeo*, 'I fear nothing but sin'.

Common Prayer. The difficulties only increased during 1661, and at the end of that year he was dismissed as the minister of Worthenbury. An arrangement was reached that he would give up his right to the annuity and also to the lease of the house, which he continued to occupy until September 1662. A curate was put into the parish and the Henry family worshipped at the church regularly and on one occasion Philip Henry was allowed to join in the Lord's Supper. He even preached in some other parishes until St Bartholomew Day, 24 August 1662.[16] This was the day that the Act of Uniformity came into force, requiring complete acceptance of the Anglican Prayer Book in every respect. He continued to attend worship at Worthenbury under his successor, even though he had to listen to sermons attacking 'false doctrine and false teachers'. He was a patient church attender, for often he had to listen to poor sermons or ones borrowed from published works. On one occasion he noted in his diary that he had been at Whitechapel 'where was good fare, thanks bee to God!' The sermon was on the Lord's Supper and it was based on 1 Corinthians 11:23. The subject was how 'the receiver takes and feedes by Faith, which in this Ordinance is all in all'. Later Philip Henry found out that the substance of the sermon had been taken from Dr Reynolds's Treatise on the Sacrament.[17]

---

16 The use of the term 'Bartholomew' was a reference to the event in France on that day in 1582 when thousands of Protestants were murdered.

17 Lee, *Diaries and Letters of Philip Henry*, p. 171.

CHAPTER 3

The Henry Family at Broad Oak

Philip Henry was forced to vacate his residence at Worthenbury after the Act of Uniformity came into force. Soon the family relocated to Broad Oak, and there Matthew Henry was born on 18 October 1662, probably prematurely. Philip Henry's diary entry included the sentences: 'We have no reason to call him Benoni—I wish we had not to call him Ichabod'.[1] The following day being the Sabbath, he was baptised in the parish church at Malpas by the rector, Rev. William Holland. Although Philip Henry wanted the sign of the cross omitted in the baptismal service, the rector insisted that it was necessary, but no godparents were involved. Because Broad Oak was Katharine's family home, and with her family's wealth coming to her, the Henry family was able to live quite well without the income from a parish appointment. This was in marked contrast to over a hundred other ministers in the area known to Philip Henry who had neither house nor income following their ejection.

---

1   Lee, *The Diaries and Letters of Philip Henry*, p. 118. Benoni – Heb. 'son of my distress' (see Gen. 35:18, in reference to Benjamin); Ichabod – Heb. 'Where is the glory?' (see 1 Sam. 4:21, in reference to the birth of a child to the wife of Phinehas after her husband's death and that of her father-in-law).

The parents both took seriously their role in the spiritual life of the children. On the occasion of his mother's death in 1707 Matthew Henry commented that his parents 'taught us the good knowledge of the Lord, of the Lord Jesus, and led us into an acquaintance with Jesus Christ, and him crucified'.[2] When he was thirteen years of age, he penned a catalogue of God's mercies to him. In it he refers to his early years in this way:

Broad Oak farmhouse, 1900, which replaced the original house that was demolished around 1746. The outbuilding on the right was essentially the same as in Philip Henry's time.

When I was born, as I have oft heard my Mother say, I was very weak, and so sickly, that most thought I could not live, yet the Lord appeared for my Deliverance; it is today thirteen years since I was born, and the Lord has preserved me ever since, blessed be his holy Name; blessed be God that I have had a good education, and was taught so earnestly to read my Bible. In the Year 1667, in *April*, Brother *John*, Sister *Sarah* and I, had all of us the Measles together; *April* 2. Brother John died, and it was thought by most that I should have died, yet contrary to the Fears of many, my Sister and I are alive,

---

2   'A Sermon Preached at Broad Oak, June 4, 1707, on the Occasion of the Death of Mrs Katharine Henry,' *The Complete Works of Matthew Henry: Treatises, Sermons and Tracts* (Grand Rapids: Baker Books, 1979), vol. II, p. 596 (henceforth cited as *The Complete Works*). The sermon can also be found in *The Life of the Rev. Philip Henry*, pp. 313-34.

blessed be Free Grace, distinguishing Mercy. *Matth.* xxiv.40. (Allusion) *One shall be taken and the other left.* The same summer I had the Ague, it hung long upon me, and yet God again delivered me.[3]

This quotation points to two aspects of Matthew Henry's early life that require further comment. First, it is clear that he was very sickly from birth, and his early years were marked by various illnesses, some of which were simply called 'ague' (fever), without any further specification to enable the naming of the precise illness. Measles often took the lives of children before inoculation was introduced, and while Matthew and Sarah recovered, their brother John died. Later in the summer of that same year Matthew had fever. He says: 'It hung long upon me, and yet God again delivered me'.[4] He had good health for a few years, and then in September 1672 he had fever again and, though very ill, he recovered.

The second aspect that needs comment is the spiritual life in his home at Broad Oak.[5] Quite apart from worship on the Lord's Day, Puritan families in general had daily times of worship and instruction within the family circle. While some households of noble Puritan families were able to employ a chaplain, most did not, and in them the father conducted family worship morning and evening. One of the Puritans, Paul Baines, advised heads of families, for the sake of the servants and children, not to pray for longer than fifteen minutes. After prayer a Bible passage was read, often accompanied by appropriate comments. Especially in morning worship the singing of a psalm was usually included. Philip Henry once said: 'Those do well that pray

---

3   William Tong, *Life of Matthew Henry* (London: Eman. Matthews, 1716), pp. 11-12. This volume is hereafter cited as *Life of Matthew Henry*.

4   Ibid., p. 12.

5   For an excellent discussion of religious life in the Puritan homes, see Elizabeth Braund, 'Daily Life among the Puritans', in D. Martyn Lloyd-Jones, ed., *Puritan Papers*, vol. 1 1956-1959 (Phillipsburg, N.J.: Presbyterian & Reformed, 2000), pp. 155-66.

morning and evening in their families, those do better that pray and read the Scriptures, but those do best that pray and read and sing the psalms'.[6] Evening worship followed much the same pattern, though the exposition of Scripture was often longer, and some catechising occurred as well.

The religious life in the Henry household, and the instruction of Matthew and his siblings, are well documented, for in writing the life of his father, Matthew set out the religious practices of his home.[7] Philip Henry led his family and servants in worship morning and evening. He recommended that the wife should sometimes pray with the husband, so that she would be familiar with leading worship in his absence, or to carry on if he died. Others he encouraged in regard to family worship, telling them that 'he who makes his house a little church, shall find that God will make it a little sanctuary'.[8] Matthew Henry's first biographer, William Tong, had known Philip and Katharine Henry, and he said that their household 'was regulated with as much Wisdom and Piety as any that our Age has produced. I have known those that upon their first Acquaintance there, were surpriz'd to see so much Beauty and Holiness, and were ready to say, *Surely God is in this Place; this is no other than the House of God and the Gate of Heaven*'.[9] John Wesley later drew attention to Philip Henry's pattern of family worship as one to be followed.[10]

Philip Henry began with a prayer asking for the help of the Holy Spirit in understanding the Scripture reading, often

---

6   Ibid., p. 159.

7   See Matthew Henry, *The Life of the Rev. Philip Henry*, pp. 72-86. For discussions on family worship among the Puritans, see Horton Davies, *The Worship of the English Puritans* (Westminster: Dacre Press, 1948), Appendix D, 'Puritan Family Worship', pp. 278-85; Leland Ryken, *Worldly Saints: The Puritans as They Really Were* (Grand Rapids: Academie Books, 1990), 'The Spiritualization of the Family', pp. 84-8.

8   Matthew Henry, *The Life of the Rev. Philip Henry*, p. 73.

9   Tong, *Life of Matthew Henry*, p. 124.

10   *Minutes of Conference*, vol. 1, p. 76 (quoted in *The Life of Rev. Philip Henry*, p. 73 fn.).

finishing the prayer with the doxology, 'unto him be glory in the church by Christ Jesus throughout all ages, world without end. Amen' (Eph. 3:21). Then a psalm was sung, usually from Barton's edition,[11] singing quickly with the use of a good variety of tunes. The Scripture reading followed, taking the Bible books in order, and accompanying the reading with a practical exposition of the passage. When he finished he would sometimes say, 'How often I have read this chapter, and never before now took notice of such a thing in it!'[12] The children were briefly questioned as to what they remembered of the reading and exposition before the family knelt for prayer. He prayed, confessing family sins and giving thanks for family mercies, mentioning specifically those in the family circle and servants and visitors who might be present in the home. At the end of the prayer he pronounced the blessing, 'The blessing of God Almighty, the Father, the Son, and the Holy Ghost, be with us all'. The children then on bended knees sought the blessing from their father and mother, and it was given even for absent members of the family – 'The Lord bless you and your brother', or, 'you and your sister that is absent'.

On Thursday evenings Philip Henry catechised both his own children and the servants on their knowledge of the Westminster Shorter Catechism, or sometimes on a book he had found helpful. On Saturday he questioned the children and servants on the passages read during the week, to see how much they remembered of them. If they had difficulty, he would explain further the passage. If visitors were present who could take part, he would involve them in this practice.

The Lord's Day was very special for Philip Henry and his family, just as it was for nearly all the Puritans from the

---

11   The psalms and hymns were printed by an Act of Parliament in October, 1645.

12   Matthew Henry, *The Life of the Rev. Philip Henry*, p. 75.

beginning of the seventeenth century.[13] While popular games, except bull- and bear-baiting, were allowed by King James's *Declaration of Sports* (1618), yet progressively the Puritan teaching on the Sabbath had its effect. Even when the Puritan influence had waned, the Parliament in 1677 confirmed the position that all ordinary callings should be set aside and the seventh day devoted to exercises aimed at 'the duties of piety and true religion, publicly and privately'. The Lord's Day for Philip Henry was a true Easter Day, and he commonly greeted his family on the Sabbath morning with the words used in the early church: *The Lord is risen; he is risen indeed.* Though the family were going out to worship in church, he had more extensive family worship than on the other days of the week. In the evening again a similar pattern of family worship took place. In further catechising the children and servants he wanted to ensure that they did not just know the words by rote, and family members repeated what they remembered of the sermons on that day. The children also reaffirmed a baptismal covenant that he composed for them, each one saying:

> I take God the Father to be my chiefest good, and highest end.
> I take God the Son to be my Prince and Saviour.
> I take God the Holy Ghost to be my Sanctifier, Teacher, Guide and Comforter.
> I take the word of God to be my rule in all my actions.
> And the people of God to be my people in all conditions.
> I do likewise devote and dedicate unto the Lord, my whole self, all I am, all I have, and all I can do.
> And this I do deliberately, sincerely, freely, and for ever.[14]

---

13 For discussions on the Puritan view of the Sabbath, see J. I. Packer, 'The Puritans and the Lord's Day', in *A Quest for Godliness: The Puritan Vision of the Christian Life* (Wheaton: Crossways Books, 1990), pp. 233-43 [this essay also appears in D. Martyn Lloyd-Jones, ed., *Puritan Papers, vol. 1*, pp. 87-99]; Leland Ryken, *Worldly Saints*, 'The Puritan Sabbath', pp. 128-32 and bibliography listed in fn. 85, p. 249.

14 Matthew Henry, *The Life of the Rev. Philip Henry*, p. 83-4.

Finally, when he prayed, he specifically included all in the household, praying 'that the ministry might in nothing be blamed' by ill conduct on the part of any. He also prayed for neighbouring towns and parishes such as Chester, Shrewsbury, Nantwich, Wrexham and Whitchurch.

While the Puritan practice of Sabbath observance has often been ridiculed, yet it was far from being a joyless day for them. They rejoiced in it, keeping it with delight. Clearly the family of Philip Henry entered into that spirit, and the same has to be said for the spiritual life and practices within the family. When Matthew was twenty years of age, he numbered and recorded the mercies he had received from God. Among other things he gave thanks:

13. That I have had, and still have Comfort more than ordinary in Relations; that I am blest with such Parents as few have, and Sisters also that I have reason to rejoice in....

15. That I have been born in a Place and Time in Gospel Light; that I have had the Scriptures, and Means for understanding them, by daily expositions and many good Books; and that I have had a heart to give my self to and delight in the Study of them....

18. That I had a Religious Education, the Principles of Religion instill'd into me with my very Milk, and from a Child have been taught the good Knowledge of God.[15]

Clearly the Henry children were brought up in a home in which there was a loving relationship between the parents. In his letters to his wife Philip Henry calls her 'Dear Heart', and writing in his diary on their wedding anniversary twenty years later he comments: 'This day we have been married twenty years, in which time we have received of the Lord more than twenty thousand mercies; to God be the glory.' He also used to say that he and his wife had been married for long and never reconciled, that is, there never was any occasion for it. Her surviving

---

15 Tong, *Life of Matthew Henry*, pp. 32-3.

letters to him were also affectionate. He was ill when away in London in 1671, and she wrote:

> I have given up all my intrest in you to my heavenly fathar and am labouring to be redy for evel tidings which if it be God knows how I shal bear it, if I should hear on thursday that you continu ill and fale to take Physigne [medicine] I shal be like to send to a plase in the Chestar choche [coach] to come to you as soone as I can .... I shal not bee content to stay from you.

She ended her letter with the words: 'My Dear Heart the lord be with you and send us a happy meeting so prayeth you faithful and loving wife, Katharine Henry.'[16]

Little is known of the domestic arrangements in the Henry household. On their marriage Katharine's father bestowed half of his estate on them, and the remainder came on his death seven years later. They had servants (both domestic and on the farm), and were able to entertain visitors, sometimes for considerable lengths of time. Philip was a neat husband about the house and grounds, so Matthew said, and though brought up in London he became a good gardener and farmer. He was noted for his kindness to the labourers he employed, as he also was to poor and distressed travellers who came near the house. If he thought he was dealing with someone who was a cheat, he would give him food or money, but then try to convince the person that they were out of God's way and could not expect His blessing.[17]

As her letters reveal, and instances in the life of the Henry family confirm, Katharine was a very sensible woman. When Matthew was considering going to Chester his father wrote:

> Your dear Mother hath no great joy in the thoughts of your Closing with them at Chester upon the termes propos'd, her reasons are weighty, & in other th.[ings] have many times sway'd with mee against my own & it hath done wel, what they are in this matter you shall hear immediately from hersf.[18]

---

16 Roberts, *Matthew Henry and His Chapel*, p. 25.

17 Matthew Henry, *The Life of the Rev. Philip Henry*, pp. 118-121.

18 Roberts, *Matthew Henry and His Chapel*, p. 21-2.

She was a devoted wife and fond mother, to whom the children were deeply attached. Katharine lived till 1707, and when she died Matthew recorded in his diary: 'This morning I received the sad tidings of my dear mother's death.' He went to Broad Oak and wrote that 'we wept and prayed together. My wife and two sisters were with my mother when she died, which was a comfort to me, though I was absent'.[19]

Matthew Henry sums up the worship in his home, and specifically the role of his father, in this way:

> He was ever carefull to have all his family present at family worship, and sometimes, living in the country, he had a great household, and he would have not only his children and domestick servants, but his workmen & day laborers, and all that were employ'd for him, if they were within call, to be present to joyn with him in that service—and many of his poor neighbours have had reason to bless God for the opportunities of that kind t^{ei} [they] have had, yet when t^{ei} must be staid for long, he would sometimes say at a night, *better one away, than all sleepy* .... He brought up his children in the fear of God and with much tenderness ....[20]

19   Matthew Henry, *The Life of the Rev. Philip Henry*, p. 337.

20   Roberts, *Matthew Henry and His Chapel*, p. 20.

CHAPTER 4

Early Education and Religious Experiences

Matthew Henry and his siblings were privileged to have their father as their principal tutor. He had had an excellent schooling and all the advantages of double degree courses at Oxford University. The children in the family were started very young on their lessons. William Tong, in the earliest biography of Matthew Henry, claims that he could read 'a Chapter in the Bible very distinctly at about three Years old, and with some Observation of what he read'.[1] While he was very young, this may well have been true, though children can often memorise passages so well that it seems as if they are reading. Philip Henry was an inventive teacher, for he even wrote an English Hebrew grammar for his daughter Sarah when she was six or seven years old. She got on so well that she could readily read a Hebrew psalm and explain the grammar of it.

In addition, Philip Henry decided to have tutors staying in the home. This was to fulfil three aims. Such a tutor could instruct the children, be a companion to Henry himself, and also be his pupil. One of the first of these tutors was William Turner, who stayed with the family on and off for three years. He first introduced Matthew to 'grammar', that is, Greek and

---

1   Tong, *Life of Matthew Henry*, p. 7.

Latin. Matthew loved his studies, but his mother worried that his health would suffer because he was constantly at his books. Even when he was very young she had to encourage him to leave his desk and get out into the fields for a walk.

The first extant letter of Matthew to his father was written in 1671, when Philip Henry was away in London. It was his own composing, as William Turner had gone to Oxford earlier in the year. Matthew reports on his studies in this way:

> Honoured Father, ever day since you went, I have done my lesson, a side of Latine, two Latine verses and two verses in grac. Test. [the Greek New Testament]. I hope I have done well, and so I will continue till you come. All my sisters (Blessed be God) are in good health, and present their duty to yourself, and service to all their Aunts, and my two little sisters desire you if you think good to buy them each of them a Bible, and if you Please Let one have marginall notes for mee, and one of my little sisters shall have mine for such a one I desire. All the rest of the family is well, and present their service to you, Longing to see you, w^ch [which] will bee very welcome to all the Family and especially to him who is and will remain,
>
> Your dutifull son and obedient servant,
>
> Matthew-Henry Matthewes.
>
> Pray pardon my scribbling.
>
> My duty to yourself and Service to all my Aunts.
>
> Pray when you come will you let us have the happiness to see my Aunt Ann with you if possible.

His mother added some words in her own distinctive style, and without finishing the sentence: 'Tel sistar Ann her nefu would fain see her that he may recover his credit lost by his ....'[2]

While Katharine came from a wealthy family, yet her spelling was always phonetic, and it is easier to read her letters aloud rather than silently. Matthew's use of the surname 'Matthewes' is interesting. It would have pleased his grandfather if he was still living, but he does not seem to have used it again. Changes

---

2   Roberts, *Matthew Henry and His Chapel*, pp. 22-3.

of surname were not unknown in this family. The name of Philip Henry's father was Henry Williams, and seemingly in accordance with an old Welsh custom, he took his father's Christian name as his surname. One of Matthew Henry's sons, Philip, did not follow in his father's religious convictions, and on becoming a Member of Parliament, assumed the name of Philip Warburton, taking his mother's maiden name as his own.

With all his education Matthew was receiving spiritual instruction from his father. The daily worship, regular catechising, and listening to his father expounding the Scriptures had their effect on him. While Philip was deprived of his living at Worthenbury, yet he was able to open the Scriptures to his own family, and on Sunday evenings some others joined the Henry family for worship in their home. When Matthew was thirteen years old he wrote a document calling it, 'A Catalogue of the Mercies of God'. After beginning by thanking God for the spiritual mercies found in Christ and the means of grace such as the Scriptures and prayer, he noted that about three years previously he began to be convinced of the truth of the gospel by hearing his father preach on Psalm 51:7: 'The sacrifices of God are a broken spirit: a broken and a contrite heart, O God, thou wilt not despise.' He says: 'I think it was that that melted me, afterwards I began to enquire after Christ.'[3]

The following year, on 7 December 1673, he heard a sermon on the marks of true grace, and had a conversation with his father about what he heard and how it applied to him personally. He had examined his own heart before God and found repentance for sin and sorrow for all that was past, though not in the measure he really desired. He continued his narrative: 'I judge myself before the Lord, blushing for shame that

---

3   Tong, *Life of Matthew Henry*, p. 8. Tong gives the whole document on pp. 8-12, while J. B. Williams, *Memoirs of the Life, Character and Writings of Matthew Henry* (orig. published 1828; reprinted Edinburgh: Banner of Truth Trust, 1974), pp. 5-6 gives part of it. Hereafter this biography is cited as *Memoirs*.

I should ever affront him as I have done; and ministers have assured me, that having repented sin and believed on Christ, I am to believe that I am pardoned; now I have done this, and I do really believe I am forgiven for Christ's sake.' He then went on to list various biblical passages, such as Isaiah 1:18, Acts 2:37-8, Acts 3:19 and 1 John 1:9, on which his profession of faith was grounded.

Matthew's siblings were also touched by the home life they enjoyed and the spiritual tone of the family. Three of them at least (Sarah, Eleanor and Ann) kept diaries. In hers, Sarah wrote about the care the parents had for them as children:

> Secured by privacy, from so much as seeing the corruptions of the world abounds with, for the first twenty years of my life I do not remember to have heard an oath, or to have seen a person drunk. But still, this was but negative religion,—the free grace of God, in infinite mercy, took early hold of me, and brought me to feel something of the powers of the world to come.[4]

While Philip Henry was not in a parish during the childhood of his children, yet there were many things to distract him from his own study and the education of the family. The church life was not conducive to his personal sense of peace, for he disagreed often with the preaching and would not take the Lord's Supper in a kneeling position. He attended the local parish church whenever a service was held, but said: 'I cannot get my heart into such a spiritual frame on Sabbath Days now, as formerly; which is both my sin and my affliction. Lord, quicken me with quickening grace!'[5] As regards the Lord's Supper, he believed that there was no warrant in Scripture for kneeling because the nature of the ordinance was a meal. Even if he had been content to kneel, he would not have done so at the rails in the church in Malpas, because they suggested that the way into the holy place had not been opened up by the work of Jesus.

---

4   Roberts, *Matthew Henry and His Chapel*, p. 21.

5   Matthew Henry, *The Life of the Rev. Philip Henry*, p. 96.

Though deprived of ministry himself, Philip Henry took his family with him to church. Many times they had a long way to go on foot to attend worship. This gave him an opportunity to talk on spiritual matters with others going and coming from services. He was generous in assessing the sermons the family heard, though sometimes he would have to say: 'That is a poor sermon indeed, out of which no good lesson may be learned.' Matthew tells us that his father often remembered some words of George Herbert (1593-1633), the poet:

> The worst speaks something good; if all want sense,
> God takes the text, and preacheth patience.[6]

Political pressure also was brought to bear on Philip Henry. In October 1663 he was taken as a prisoner to Hanmer, along with several fellow ministers. After a few days they were examined as to their part in some suspected plot against the Government and allowed them to return to their homes. In 1665 Philip Henry was appointed a sub-collector of taxes for the township of Hanmer. The attempt was being made in this way to suggest to the public that Philip Henry was only a layman, not a minister. Later in the same year he was again brought to the gaol, this time because of his attendance at private meetings, and because it was claimed that he was administering the Lord's Supper. When the authorities realised that they could not pin anything on him, he was released on a bond of £20 on condition that he returned to gaol if notice was given, and that he had to live *peaceably*! The time in gaol must not have been too strict

---

6   Ibid., p. 102. The lines come from stanza 72 of 'The Church-porch'. Both father and son clearly were very familiar with Herbert's poems, and both quote them on occasion. For Matthew Henry, see for example, Allan M. Harman, ed., *The Unpublished Sermons of Matthew Henry on the Covenant of Grace* (Fearn: Christian Focus Publications, 2004), p. 111. Herbert also had as appreciative readers of his poems Richard Baxter, William Cowper and John Wesley. For a short account of Herbert's life see, *George Herbert of Bemerton: A Selection from 'The Temple', with an Introduction by Frances Forrest* (Bemerton Rectory, Salisbury, n.d.).

because Philip and his companions 'had prayer and conference together', to their mutual edification.[7]

A somewhat greater test came in 1666, when the Five Mile Act came into operation. The intention of this act was to ensure the nonconformist ministers did not come or stay within five miles (8.3 km) of their former parishes. The family's Broad Oak residence was reputed to be only four miles (6.6 km) from the nearest part of the boundary of his former parish at Worthenbury. Philip Henry got it measured and it was five miles and 600 yards (8.9 km). To make sure that there was no claim against him, he left his family and for a year he went to live with friends. He redeemed the time by helping those friends in spiritual matters, and later found he could return home with impunity.

Certainly Matthew Henry saw and heard much of his father's practice in expounding Scripture, as well as being exposed to many other preachers and visitors to the home. In various ways Philip Henry encouraged the spiritual lives of his children. He directed them to spend an hour every Saturday afternoon in religious exercises in order to prepare for the following Lord's Day, and this time of worship was led by Matthew. This leadership role among his own siblings seems to have been an indication of the way in which his mind and heart were moving in relation to the ministry. From a young age he would join with groups of Christians to discuss spiritual issues and to pray together. At times, too, he had the opportunity to explain the chapter of the Bible that was read. This was done without any sense of pride on his part. Another thing that Philip Henry encouraged his children to do was to listen to sermons and then writes notes of them. Matthew continued this practice throughout his life and tried to follow the advice of one of his father's friends. This was to the effect that if there was *chaff* in a sermon, that was what people normally carried away. Instead, the recommendation was to take *bread* from it.

---

7   Matthew Henry, *The Life of the Rev. Philip Henry*, p. 106.

At the age of seven, Ann Henry took part in repeating the main points of sermons in the family circle, 'having the happiness of a very quick understanding, and a good memory', according to her brother Matthew.[8] At the age of eleven she began to keep notes of sermons in a book, and continued this practice until her death. She also wrote out her father's expositions of Scripture given at family worship, and used them in conjunction with her own Bible reading.[9] Later she frequently picked up those earlier notes and used them. One Sunday when she was not at church, she wrote: 'This day I spent at home: reviewed over some sermons I had writ from my father three years ago concerning the several steps of Christ's exaltation.' The fact that Philip Henry did not believe in destroying any of his sermon notes made possible a wide distribution of them among family and friends.

The diaries of Matthew's sisters were almost exclusively devoted to religious entries.[10] They were different from their father's diary which was more comprehensive in scope, involving matters such as business affairs or political issues of the day. Matthew and his three sisters all made public profession of faith and were admitted to the Lord's Table when they were sixteen or seventeen years of age.

So Matthew's home education continued till his late teens. He professed personal faith in the Saviour, and his life commended itself to his parents and other friends. Those who knew him thought that in the future he would grow to be a notable Christian and that his gifts would be used in the service of God's church.

---

8   J. B. Williams, *Memoirs of the Life & Character of Mrs Sarah Savage: To Which are added, Memoirs of Her Sister, Mrs Hulton* (London: Holdsworth and Ball, 1828), p. 286.

9   Ibid., p. 294.

10   For Sarah, see J. B. Williams, *Memoirs of the Life & Character of Mrs Sarah Savage*, especially 'Chapter IV Miscellaneous Extracts from her Diary between the years 1688 and 1732', pp. 141-224; for Eleanor, ibid., pp. 264-76; for Ann, ibid., pp. 277-344.

At first Philip Henry doubtless considered that, like himself, his son Matthew would go to university, most probably following in his footsteps and attending Oxford. However, as the years went by he realised that the universities had changed, as the Christian presence and influence had lessened since his own student days. While he had early on encouraged his friends to send their sons to university, later he changed his mind. He wanted to spare his own son Matthew from the snares and temptations at university, and hence kept him at home till he was almost eighteen. At that age, probably because he felt that he had done as much as he could for Matthew's education, he decided to send him to London to attend the dissenting academy run by Rev. Thomas Doolittle (1630–1707). Academies such as this one were illegal institutions set up to enable boys from nonconformist homes to obtain the equivalent of a university education. In fact, they became more rigorous in their teaching than the universities of Oxford or Cambridge, and in particular they pioneered instruction in English at a tertiary level. Many of these academies also had in view the preparation of young men for the ministry, and in the course of time they became theological colleges preparing students for ministry in nonconformist churches.[11]

---

11   For more information on the dissenting academies, see Irene Parker, *Dissenting Academies in England: Their Rise and Progress and Their Place among the Educational Systems of the Country* (orig. published in 1914; reprinted in New York, 1969); Ashley J. W. Smith, *Birth of Modern Education: The Contribution of the Dissenting Academies, 1600-1800* (London: Independent Press, 1954).

CHAPTER 5

His Studies in London

It was in July 1680 that Matthew Henry went to London to begin a new phase of his education under the supervision of Dr Thomas Doolittle.[1] He was accompanied by his father, and by an older relative, Robert Bosier, who had been living with the Henry family at Broad Oak. After study at St Edmund Hall in Oxford, where he had been a commoner, Robert had come to prepare better for 'holy orders' by spending some time with the Henry family, doubtless to benefit from Philip Henry's tuition. Though Robert Bosier was older than Matthew, a strong bond of friendship developed between them and they were delighted to have each other's company both on the journey and during the stay in London.

Matthew wrote a letter to his sisters describing the trip to London: The journey took five days, and here are some sections of his letter:

Dear sisters,

I came safe, through the good providence of God, upon Friday last into London, and have reason to say, 'It is of the Lord's mercies that I am not consumed:' for he 'holdeth my soul in life,' and 'keepeth all my bones'... . Well then, on Munday wee baited [took refreshment] at Newport and came through Tong to Wolverhampton y[superscript t] [that] night about sunsett.

---

1   Dr Thomas Doolittle (1630-1707) had been converted as a boy in Kidderminster under the preaching of Richard Baxter (1615-1691).

From thence we set out next morning about six or 7 of clock, & came through Bromicham[2] to Henley (y^t was 20 miles from Wolverhamton) and there we baited, and lay at Stratford upon Avon (y^t was but 5 miles from Henley). On Wednesday morning wee came from Stratford to Shipston, thence to Longcompton, thence to Enston, where we baited, and then came to Oxford between five and six. At Oxford I saw the judges come in, Sir Job [Charleton] for one, and next morning heard the assize sermon, at St. Mary's. It was preached by one Mr Lessy, a young man. The text was Hos. iv.1, 2, 3.... On Thursday, about three o'clock we set out from Oxford.

The letter continues with reference to sights in London that impressed the young scholar. He commented on the number of coaches he saw (over a hundred), and that a day or two later he went to see Bedlam, the asylum for the mentally ill, and then the monument marking where the great fire of London commenced. From the top of the 345 steps of the monument, he notes the view he had of the whole city. The Lord's Day was busy, with morning worship at Dr Doolittle's church, and afternoon worship there as well, but with Philip Henry preaching on Lamentations 3:22: 'It is of the Lord's mercies that we are not consumed, because his compassions fail not.' Along with his cousin Robert he even attended another service at 5 p.m., when a young minister, Mr John Shower, preached, but the crowd was so great they could 'scarce get any room'.

A brief reference is made to where he is going to study:

This morning wee went and first bought a couple of Trunks, putt all our things in them, and then went along with y^m [them] to

---

2   Williams, *Memoirs*, p. 10 gives this as Birmingham, but Brummagem must be intended. While Williams is correct in understanding this as Birmingham, yet the use of the alternative word is significant. In the seventeenth-century Birmingham was noted for the production of counterfeit coins, and Brummagem came to be used in reference to the town, and it also became a word that is still in use to describe what is spurious or showy. 'Brummie' came to describe a person from Birmingham.

Islington, where I saw yᵉ [the] place wee are like to abide in, and
do perceive that our rooms are likely to be very strait [narrow]
and little. That Mr Doolittel is very studious and diligent and that
Mrs Doolittel and her daughter are very fine and gallant.[3]

Little is known about the actual studies that Matthew Henry
did at the academy. He was part of a group of students who
numbered about thirty. Two contemporaries commented much
later on their knowledge of him from those days. Rev. Samuel
Bury, who came from the same part of England and knew the
Henry family when he was only a schoolboy, met up again with
Matthew at Islington. His recollection was this, that he:

> was never better pleas'd while he was at Mr Doolittle's, than
> when he was in young Mr Henry's Company; he had such
> a Savour of Religion always upon his Spirit, was of such
> a cheerful Temper, so diffusive of all Knowledge, so ready in
> the Scripture, so pat in all his Petitions in every Emergency,
> so full and clear in all his Performances, abating that at first
> he had almost an unimaginable Quickness of Speech, which
> afterwards he corrected, as well for his own sake, as for the
> benefit of others. He was to me a most desirable Friend, and
> I have Heaven the better since he went thither.[4]

Similar testimony came from Rev. Henry Chandler, later minister at Bath. He recalled his time with Matthew Henry in these
words:

> It is now 35 years since I had the happiness of being in the
> same House with Mr Henry, so that it is impossible I should
> recollect the several passages that fix'd in me such an honour-
> able idea of him, that nothing can efface while Life and Rea-
> son lasts; this I perfectly well remember, that for serious Piety,
> and the most obliging Behaviour, he was universally belov'd
> by all the House; we were, I remember near 30 Pupils when
> Mr Henry grac'd and enterain'd the Family, and I remember

---

3   Roberts, *Matthew Henry and His Chapel*, p. 41.

4   Tong, *Life of Matthew Henry*, p. 29.

not that ever I heard one of the Number speak a Word to his Disparagement; I am sure it was the common Opinion, that he was as sweet temper'd, courteous, and obliging a Gentleman as could come into a House; his going from us was universally lamented.[5]

The final sentence of that quotation refers to Matthew Henry's departure from the academy. What happened was that many of the students caught some sort of fever, including Matthew and his 'cousin', Robert Bosier. Philip Henry had either stayed in London or gone home and then went away to Boreatton, for he had no regular congregational commitments calling him back to Broad Oak. On 19 August 1680, he wrote to his daughter Sarah and in reference to Matthew he says: 'We are in hopes to hear, his Ague hath left him, or, however dealt more gently with him, but however the event bee his will be done, whose we are, and whom we serve ....'[6]

What transpired was that both Matthew and Robert Bosier were among those who were taken ill. Matthew seemed to get better, but then had a relapse. When he was recovering his father wrote encouraging him to return home, saying that if that happened then it would be a case of 'man purposes but God disposes'. The illness turned out differently for Robert, and he succumbed to the fever, dying along with many others in London – at least 800 in the same week. He died 'a hopeful yong man, serious & religious'.[7] Philip Henry goes on in his diary to record that Robert was buried in the new churchyard near the artillery ground, and his thoughts were with his son in his sadness. He wrote: 'And now my dear child his Alter Idem [other self] is left in widowhood and besides, not well, when wee heard y[e] [the] tidings which was at y[e] [the] time of morning Family worship, it caus'd a wett prayer amongst us'.[8]

---

5   Ibid., pp. 29-30.

6   Roberts, *Matthew Henry and His Chapel*, p. 43.

7   Lee, *Diaries and Letters of Philip Henry*, p. 293.

8   Ibid., p. 294.

Two of Matthew Henry's biographers consider it likely that he stayed on in London at Dr Doolittle's academy until 1682, and this has been repeated by many since.[9] However, Philip Henry's diary makes it plain that Matthew returned to Broad Oak on 25 September 1680. While glad that sufficient strength had been given to their son to make the journey, yet the father notes that 'in a short time was the Lord pleas'd to ruffle and overturn what wee had long purpos'd and design'd hoping it might have been for good, but hee gives not account of any of his matter'. Their relief that Matthew was well enough to come back home was tempered by sadness that the plan for him to study with Dr Doolittle came to such a sudden and unexpected end. Later entries in his diary (for 9 June 1681 and 10 June 1682) confirm that Matthew was at home at Broad Oak, not in London.[10]

His education continued at home under his father's careful eye, and it is clear that much of his knowledge, including the Latin classics, was passed on to his son. Spiritually Matthew grew further during this period, which was to extend from 1681 to 1687. On 16 October 1681, his nineteenth birthday, he drew up another record of 'Mercies Received'. After giving thanks for being created with an immortal soul and with a body neither blind nor deaf nor dumb, he goes on to list and enumerate the temporal blessings he has received.[11] These included:

---

9   William Tong, op. cit., p., 30 and J. B. Williams, op. cit., p. 13, though the latter is more reserved on the matter, saying that 'how long Mr Henry continued at this seminary is not easily discoverable'. P. O. Williams, *Matthew Henry* (London: The Presbyterian Historical Society of England, 1926), p. 6, correctly says: 'Nearly all the students suffered at the same time with the same fever, with the result that Matthew Henry was home again in two months, his London Theological course at an end.'

10 Dr Doolittle was persecuted by the authorities and had to move first to Battersea, and then to Clapham, where he dispersed his students among various families.

11 The full text is given in Tong, *Life of Matthew Henry*, pp. 30-4, and Williams, *Memoirs*, pp. 13-16.

7. That I have been ever since [birth] comfortably provided for with Bread to eat, and Raiment to put on, not for Necessity only, but for Ornament and Delight, and that without any Pains and Care ....

11. Thus I have had comfortable Accommodation, as to House, Lodging, Fuel, &c. and have been a Stranger to the Wants of many Thousands in that kind.

12. That I was born to a Competency of Estate in the World, so that (as long as God pleases to continue it) I am likely to be on the giving, and not on the receiving hand.

13. That I have had, and still have Comfort more than ordinary in Relations; that I am blest with such Parents as few have, and sisters also that I have reason to rejoice in.

14. That I have had a liberal Education, having a Capacity for, and been bred up to the Knowledge of the Language, Arts and Sciences, and that through God's Blessing on my Studies, I have made some Progress therein.

15. That I have been born in a Place and Time of Gospel Light; that I have had the Scriptures, and Means for understanding them, by daily Expositions and many good Books; and that I have had a Heart to give my self to and delight in the study of them.

This catalogue of blessings serves to emphasise the family circle that meant so much to Matthew Henry. His relationships with parents and siblings were particularly close and loving, while his privileged position had enabled him to pursue his studies without worry or financial concerns. His comment that he had 'made some progress' in his studies is a major understatement.

One particular statement confirms what had been evident earlier in his life, and that is his intention to dedicate himself to the Christian ministry. This is what he wrote: 'That God hath inclined my heart to devote and dedicate myself to him, and to his service, and the service of his church in the work of the ministry, if ever he shall please to use me.' While resident at home he was not only having the opportunity to study with his father, but also to see his father's pastoral gifts in operation, and to a limited extent to listen to him preaching. The father's diaries also made it plain that Matthew on some occasions went with him as he fulfilled engagements elsewhere.

One of Philip Henry's close friends was Richard Hunt, of Boreatton, Shropshire. The Hunt family looked on him as their pastor, and once a quarter he was with them for a Lord's Day and on it he observed the Lord's Supper. When he came back from London, Matthew was often among those who went there for spiritual refreshment, and Richard Hunt also served as an adviser to him. One piece of advice concurred with Philip Henry's own view. He had earlier considered sending his son to Oxford or Cambridge, but the altered views in the universities, and the fact that nonconformists could not enrol in theology or philosophy, meant that he came to the position that Matthew should go rather to London and study law at Gray's Inn. No indication exists that his parents, and his father in particular, thought of this as being anything other than some further liberal arts training.

Matthew took the advice of his father and Mr Hunt, and proceeded again to London in April 1685. In the first letter his father wrote to him after he went back to London he conveyed the prayer that God would direct him. He wishes to hear that his son has not forgotten the rules given to him, and that he will 'consult health & wholesomness, conveniency & honesty'. He ends the letter by wishing that his son could share in some of the sweet air of Broad Oak perfumed by the blossoms of early summer rather than the offensive smells of London. The parental advice was to arm himself against such smells until he got used to them![12]

---

12   Lee, *Diaries and Letters of Philip Henry*, p. 337.

On this occasion his studies moved in a different direction. He looked into the nature of divine and human laws, and enjoyed study of civil law and the various laws affecting municipal affairs. Some of his friends were worried with his interest in law, for they thought that this meant that he was going to abandon any inclination to enter the ministry. His father made this comment in a letter to him: 'It is the talk and wonder of many of our friends what we mean by this sudden change of your course and way: but I hope, through God's goodness and mercy, they will shortly see it was for good.' That Philip Henry had some concerns for his son's spiritual life in London was made plain at the conclusion of the same letter:[13]

> Be careful, my dear child, in the main matter. Keep yourself always in the love of God, let nothing come, however not abide, as a cloud between you and his favour, for in that is *life*. Rejoice in the great auction, and make the Pearl of Price sure, and the field too in which it is. Farewell. Much love is to you from all here, and particularly from
>
> Your loving father,
>
> P. H.

But such fears were groundless. Though studying at Holborn Court, Gray's Inn, he found several others who shared his interest in spiritual matters and he entered into discussions with them, and at times he expounded the Scriptures. Four years had now elapsed since he had had the brief period at Dr Doolittle's academy. As the Catholic James II was now on the throne, the times did not allow unhindered ministerial training for dissenters. It is apparent that Matthew Henry's going to Gray's Inn and studying law was a 'safe' course of action. Law was open to dissenters, public ministry was not.

More than once in his letters his father referred to the fact that not many of the family's friends were able to find where Matthew was living. He recognised, though, that this could be

---

13   Williams, *Memoirs*, pp. 19-20.

a blessing, enabling his son to get on with his studies, and comments on 'a good Item written over a studious Person's study door *Amice, quisquis*'. These Latin words form the opening of some lines used by various scholars in the Reformation and post-Reformation periods:

> Amice, quisquis huc venis,
> > Aut agito paucis, aut abi,
> > Aut me laborantem adjuva.

> Friend, who comes here to stay,
> > Be brief, or go away I pray,
> > Or help me while I work today.

Matthew was further advised by his father that 'a good Book is a good companion at any time, but especially a good God, who is always ready to hold communion with those that desire & seek communion with him'.[14]

The time in London also provided opportunities for wider education, perhaps with a view to being able to gain some employment as a language teacher. With two others he enrolled as a student of French with Dr Du Viel. For three months he attended classes of two hours' duration at 2 p.m. on Monday, Wednesday and Friday. At the end of this period he wrote that he had progressed so far with his study that he had 'insight into the French, as, with a little help of a Dictionary, to read with understanding any thing ordinary in the language'. One of his sisters, Katharine, picked up on his reference to obtaining employment through his French studies and she wrote humorously on behalf of her sisters: '*We* shall be very ambitious to be your scholars to learn French; but I think they say *one* tongue is enough for a woman.' His father was more practical in his advice. In a discussion with the Bishop of St Asaph words were quoted from a French catechism, and Philip Henry was unable to check on the accuracy of the translation. Hence he encouraged his son to set his mind to his present French studies, 'as

---

14   Lee, *Diaries and Letters of Philip Henry*, p. 344.

wil make it easy for you to proceed in it yourself afterwards but remember always, Omnia σύν θεῷ [All things (are possible) with God]'.[15]

This same letter appears to have been a joint effort by the family, for his mother adds her parental admonition, encouraging him to live a godly life:[16]

Dear Child,

It is much my comfort and rejoicing to hear so often from you, and, although I have little to send you but love, and my blessing, your father being absent, I write a line or two to you to mind you to keep in touch with God, as I hope you do, by solemn, secret, daily prayer; watching therein with perseverance; not forgetting what you have been taught, and the covenant engagements, renewed again and again, that you lie under, to walk circumspectly, in your whole conversation: watching against youthful lusts, evil company, sins, and snares from the world, and the devil.

Your affectionate Mother,
K. H.[17]

It must have been encouraging to all the family to receive the constant stream of letters from Matthew in London. In one of them he reflected on the speedy way that news came to him from home, for he said, 'a letter can come from your hands to mine, through the hands of so many who are strangers to us both, in the space of sixty hours'. He took up this idea of speedy access and turned it into comments on our approach to God.

But as ready as this way is, blessed be God, we have a readier way to send to Heaven at all hours; and can convey our letters

15   Ibid., p. 347.

16   Williams, *Memoirs*, pp. 23-4.

17   Someone must have edited this letter as it does not have the usual idiosyncrasies of spelling. Most probably it was J. B. Williams who performed this task.

thither, and receive gracious answers thence in less time than
so. That the throne of grace is always open to which we have
(how sweet a word it is) τὴν παρρησίαν—'liberty of speech,'
when we are with him and more so, τὴν προσαγωγὴν ἐν
πεποιθήσει, Eph. iii.12. *We have access with confidence*; we are
introduced by the Spirit, as ambassadors conducted to the
Prince by the master of the ceremonies. Esther had access
to Ahasuerus, but not access with confidence; far from it,
when she said I will go in, and if I perish, I perish. But we
have access with confidence, through the 'new and living way'
laid open for us to the Father, by the blood of his Son, who
ever lives to make intercession, in the virtue and value of
his satisfaction. And if this be not sufficient ground for that
πεποίθησις—confidence—what is?[18]

At this period in England the Anglican churches were the only
authorised ones, and the dissenters had to be careful regarding
the practice of their faith. This was the peak period of persecution of them. Matthew chose to go to the Anglican churches
both on the Lord's Day and during the week. He heard Dr Still-
ingfleet at St Andrews, Holborn, and Dr Tillotson at Lawrence
Jury, both of whom were good preachers. However, even good
preaching did not make up for the loss of 'Broad Oak Sab-
baths', as he called the Lord's Days at his home.

During these studies in London, he wrote twice a week to
his parents, and received one letter a week from his father. Even
in letter writing great care was needed. In one of those letters,
his father reflects on the dangers for himself and others, and
how careful he had to be lest suspicion fall on him. On 20 June
1685, Philip Henry wrote this to his son in London:

Wee did not go to Rhuabon on Wednesd.[ay] in regard to the
discomposures that were in the Neighborhood, which are
now allay'd, upon occasion of the D.[uke] of M.[onmouth]'s

---

18   Williams, *Memoirs*, p. 21. It is interesting that he was so familiar with the
     Greek text of the New Testament that he slips Greek words into his
     letters, though often giving the English translation immediately.

invasion & the proclaiming of him Trayt[r]. [traitor] which the Post before brought tidings of; I keep home, hear little, & say less; 'Tis our unhappiness, to bee suspected p.[er]sons without cause, & to be expos'd accordingly, though quiet in the land.[19]

Philip Henry's comments are very revealing for they show the need for great care on the part of dissenters. At this time John Howe, minister of the Presbyterian congregation meeting in the Haberdasher's Hall in Staining Lane, London, was over on the Continent. He left suddenly without telling his congregation. In the letter they received from him after his departure, he told his congregation how much ill-health came to him because someone like him could not walk the London streets in the daytime.[20] The danger was not just perceived as being possible. Philip Henry and others knew what it was to be put in prison. For in company with six ministers from Lancashire, Philip Henry was placed in custody in Chester Castle for three weeks. Matthew was at home at the time and said in a letter to his father:

I am very sorry I cannot come to see you, indeed many of my friends are against it and therefore I submit, hoping and praying & waiting for a comfortable meeting in God's due time, and yet am apt to think I could come without danger.[21]

From there he wrote to his wife, 'Dear Heart', warning of 'further sufferings' and specifically sending his love to Matthew and giving some directions. He wrote:

Our Gards change every howr, which makes it so very hard to come to us, else wee might oblige them. I would gladly see him, but when, or how I know not, I think there's little danger of any harm to him here, if there bee none at home, at his return.[22]

---

19   Lee, *Diaries and Letters of Philip Henry*, p. 338.

20   E. Calamy, *Memoirs of the Life of the late Revd Mr John Howe* (London: Sam Chandler, 1724), pp. 113-125.

21   Lee, *Diaries and Letters of Philip Henry*, p. 339.

22   Ibid., p. 341.

Later that same year Philip Henry wrote to his son: 'Your letter escaped opening, write, but bee cautious what & how.'[23] The replies were, to use William Tong's words,

> full of expressions of affection and tender duty to his good parents, and most tender respect to his sisters; he used to give his father an account of all remarkable occurrences, which he did with great judgment and exactness, and yet with all the caution the difficulties of the time required.[24]

It is probable that in addition to his twice-weekly letters, Matthew forwarded a summary of events in London to his family. This is shown by the fact that writing on 17 November 1685 he included reference to visiting Rev. Richard Baxter, but the letter contained no account of public events. However, another document of the same date gave considerable news of what was happening in London. The family valued the correspondence so much that they copied them into a book, the first few showing his father's handwriting and then that of one of his sisters. He recounts among other things the trial of those involved in the uprisings led by the Dukes of Argyll and Monmouth, and events in the Parliament such as the King's speech regarding the little help he got from the militia during the rebellions. He also informs them of recent events in France, writing:

> London, Dec. 8, '85 Peace & safety are great mercyes & to bee more prized when our Brethren abroad especially in France are in trouble & Great Distress, great beyond expression. Every week wee hear worse & worse tidings concerning them. Those y^t [that] fled out of y^e [the] Country are now commanded to return by such a time, or else bee proclaimed Traytors & their estates confiscate. Y^y [they] y^t [that] will not go to Mass by such a day must go to Prison—and there what hardships they endure cannot bee conceived. Those that have bin forced to Mass as many thousands have by great violence (& troubled

---

23   Ibid., p. 343.

24   Tong, *Life of Matthew Henry*, p. 51.

for it) if any of y^m [them] fall sick neigbors must give notice
to the Parish Priest (& are to be punished if they do not) y^e
[the] Priest tenders them then Sacrm.^{r} [sacrament] & extreme
unction which if they refuse how sick soever they been they
are hurried to the jaol. If they dye, theres the end of y^m. If
they recover they are hanged.[25]

Three months later Matthew again comments on the situation
in France in these words:

Troubles in France continue and increase. An Edict that all
protestants must abjure within a week or their estates con-
fiscated & they sent to ye Gallyes. One wrote over lately y^t
of one Church formerly consisting of 6,000 there is but 40
remaining but what are dead, fled or abjur'd. He was one of
the 40 & dragooners quartered upon him, so y^t hee had much
adoe to hold out. Divers sad storyes are told. It is said wee
shall have a Publick Collection for their relief by Authority.[26]

While Matthew Henry makes no mention of listening to dissenting preachers, yet he certainly had contacts with fellow
nonconformists. Once a week, on an afternoon, six or eight
theological students gathered together for discussions, and he
joined them. They were students of Rev. Charles Morton whose
training school had been dispersed. Matthew was in London
when the very prominent nonconformist, Richard Baxter, was
tried at the Guildhall. He was found guilty and sentenced to
pay 500 merks, to stay in prison till they were paid, and to be
on a good behaviour bond for seven years.

Matthew Henry was able to visit Richard Baxter. He had
tried previously to do so but found him busy. When he saw
him, he reported to his father, he was 'in pretty comfortable
circumstances, though a prisoner, in a private home near the
prison, attended on by his own man, and maid'. He found him

---

25   These, and further selections from this notebook, can be found in
     Roberts, *Matthew Henry and His Chapel*, pp. 53-71.

26   Ibid., p. 71.

looking better than when he saw him last (but does not mention when that was). Most probably Matthew was encouraged by his father to visit Richard Baxter, for he took a monetary gift from Philip Henry. Matthew's account of handing over the gift was couched in this way: 'The token you sent he would by no means be persuaded to accept of, and was almost angry when I pressed it, from one outed as well as himself. He said he did not use to receive; and I understand since, his need is not great.'[27]

Some other things about the visit were also related to his father. He had spent about an hour with Richard Baxter, and was accompanied by a good friend, Samuel Lawrence, afterwards a nonconformist minister. Richard Baxter approved of what Matthew Henry was doing in regard to studies, and commented that young men could get as much out of this type of study as by travelling abroad. He enquired after Shropshire friends and sent his respects to Philip Henry. In addition, he gave his two young visitors some warning. They should:

> prepare for trials, and said the best preparation for them was a life of faith, and a constant course of self-denial. He thought it harder constantly to deny temptations to sensual lusts and pleasures, than to resist one single temptation to deny Christ for fear of suffering: the former requiring such constant watchfulness; however, after the former, the latter will be the easier.[28]

The spiritual state of Matthew Henry towards the close of his time in London can be gauged by a letter he wrote to a friend, George Illidge, of Nantwich. George's heart had been opened when very young, and though he was the only one in his family

---

27 Williams, *Memoirs*, p. 22. Philip Henry may well have assisted many other ministers by giving gifts and so helping to support them and their families. Baxter's reference to 'outed' is to the Great Ejection of 1662. He was objecting to taking financial assistance from a fellow minister who was also 'outed' at that time.

28 Ibid., p. 22.

to follow Christ, he grew spiritually through attending the meetings that Philip Henry conducted at Broad Oak.

Matthew claims to be writing while indisposed, and so had 'written confusedly', but the letter is just as straightforward and organised as any of his letters or other writings. He sets out ten great principles that he had been thinking about and which he believed would be of great use to a Christian and influential in directing practical conduct. These included the biblical teaching that all we do is open to the eye of God, and that we have to live up to gospel privileges, 'living up to Gospel Love as well as Gospel light'. He wrote of us being 'in this World as an Inn, and must be gone shortly', and if our present lodging is hard and cold, 'it is no great matter, our Lodging in our Father's House will be soft and warm enough'.

He concluded the letter with the thought that Christians have to be concerned with the spiritual state of their neighbours:

> If there be any that are asking the Way to Zion, with their Faces thitherward, pray tell them the Way. Tell them,
>
> 1. There is but one Gate into this Way, and that is the straight Gate of sound Conversion.
>
> 2. Tell them that Way is narrow, that there is not Elbow-room for their Lusts, let them know the worst of it; and that those that would be good Soldiers of Christ must endure Hardness.
>
> 3. Tell them, notwithstanding this, it is a Way of Pleasantness; it gives spiritual, though it prohibits sensual Pleasures.
>
> 4. Tell them there is Life Eternal at the End, and let them be assured that one Hour of Joy in Heaven, will make 'em amends for an Age of Trouble upon Earth; one Sheaf of that Harvest will be Recompence enough for a Seedness of Tears, Psal. cxxvi.5, 6.[29]

---

29   The full text of the letter is given in Tong, *Life of Matthew Henry*, pp. 42-8.

As his time at Gray's Inn came to a close in June 1686, Matthew was well prepared for the next stage of his life. He could look back on years of study with his father, the short period with Dr Doolittle and the year at Gray's Inn itself. He had the three languages most needed – Greek, Hebrew and Latin – and also some proficiency in French. He had read widely in theology, and was able to express himself very ably with his pen. In speech, at first he was unimaginably quick, as one of his fellow students at the academy recalled,[30] but he learnt how to overcome this. His departure from London in June 1686 meant that he could now turn his mind to future ministry, and he was not long back home at Broad Oak before, in God's providence, he was led to Chester. The legacy of his years in London stayed with him, for at times in his commentary he used legal sayings to make a point, giving Latin with an English translation. Thus in writing about Ahab's guilt over Naboth's death and entering into possession of his vineyard (1 Kings 21:18), he wrote: 'By taking possession, he avowed all that was done, and made himself *ex post facto*—as an accessory after the fact.'[31]

---

30   Ibid., p. 29.

31   This example is taken from J. P. Thackway, 'Matthew Henry and His Commentary', *Bible League Quarterly* 376 (January-March 1994), p. 281.

CHAPTER 6

Ministerial Calling and Settlement at Chester

In June 1686, Matthew Henry returned to his parents' home at Broad Oak and spent some months there. It was soon apparent that his second stay in London, and his legal studies, had not diverted his interest away from the Christian ministry. He took whatever opportunity that arose to preach, so testing his gifts for the ministry, and his hearers were blessed through that preaching and encouraged him in the work of the gospel.

During that visit home he spent some days at Nantwich with George Illidge, who had not received much spiritual help in his own home. He was greatly assisted by Matthew Henry's preaching and conversation, and was a regular and welcome visitor at Broad Oak. George was concerned about the spiritual life of his neighbours at Nantwich and invited his friend to come to preach in his home. This he did to considerable groups of people. Some came out of curiosity, and having lived 'very loose and profligate lives' (as William Tong described them) were startled by his preaching. On the last occasion he preached, the text was from Job 37:22: 'With God is terrible majesty.' George Illidge noticed a man present who was notorious for his godless life. Next morning he called to see what the impact of the sermon had been, only to find the man and his wife were in tears. Conviction of his sins caused the man to weep, while his wife wept because she saw her husband weeping! He was in great distress, but George Illidge spoke and prayed with him. The man taught his wife to read and commenced family worship. Some time later his wife died, but before that she gave every evidence of having experienced a true conversion. However, despite all the spiritual prospects for the husband, he ultimately fell away from the faith.

These experiences deepened Matthew Henry's sense of call to the Christian ministry. He went to Chester but did not divulge the reason for this visit. In his description of the congregation to which he later ministered, 'A Short Account of the Beginning and Progress of Our Congregation',[1] he simply says that:

> about the end of the year 1686 some business drew me to Chester, and I lodg'd at Mr Henthorn's who a little before had been at Broad-Oke on a Lord's Day and understood that I sometimes preach'd, and therefore urg'd me to preach at his house in the evening, which I did two or three times; I also preached at Mr Harvy's, and once at Mr Jolly's, and had the happiness of contracting an intimate acquaintance with that worthy and pious Gentleman Mr Edward Greg, a man of an excellent and sweet temper, and great usefulness.[2]

The dissenters there, having heard of Henry's presence, sought the opportunity to hear him preach at various house meetings. No liberty yet existed for formal preaching in a church or chapel, but for several evenings he preached in three houses. Those who heard him made it clear that they wanted him to come to Chester as their minister. They had lost by death two aged ministers within the previous two years, Rev. William Cook, and Rev. Ralph Hall. Another minister, Rev. John Harvey, though well advanced in years, still continued a ministry but in a very

1 The account is printed in Roberts, *Matthew Henry and His Chapel*, pp. 72-101.

2 Ibid., pp. 75-6.

private way, and not all the followers of the other two ministers had joined with his hearers.

Rumours circulated late in 1686 that the Government was going to give permission for the dissenters to worship openly. This encouraged the people in Chester who had heard Matthew Henry preach to seek to have him as their pastor. Mr Henthorn and Mr Greg came to Broad Oak in January 1687 with the request that, if that freedom for the dissenters did eventuate, he would come as their pastor. He was then twenty-five years old; he believed that God had led him to Chester in His good providence, and discussions with his father seem to have confirmed his sense of call. He encouraged the people, but made two conditions: he would only come if Mr Harvey gave his consent, and also he wished to return to London for some months. Both conditions were acceptable to his future parishioners.

No clear statement exists as to why he wanted to return to London, but certain facts point to his reasons. First of all, he was waiting to see if the rumours were confirmed concerning the relaxation of the prohibition on nonconformists meeting together openly for worship. Late in 1686 a licence system was introduced whereby dissenters could exempt themselves, by payment of a fee, from prosecution because they failed to attend an Anglican church or instead practised their own religious beliefs. Not many applied for licences, but by February and March 1687 in many places dissenting congregations were openly worshipping. Writing to his father, Matthew reported that hundreds were attending the preaching of Mr Faldo, a Congregationalist minister, at Mr Slater's meeting house in Moorfields. Then the King's Proclamation of Indulgence was issued on 4 April 1687. This indulgence was intended by the King to favour Roman Catholicism, but Matthew Henry pointed out that it was:

> wonderfully over-ruled by the Divine Providence not only to
> the Relief and Comfort of many good People then in Prison,

and otherwise in Distress, but to the Advancement of the Interests of Religion in the Nation; and was likewise such a Provocation to many of the Ch[urch]. of E[ngland], that it was the first thing and an Inlet to other things that made them uneasy at King James and his Government, and prepared the way for the glorious Revolution.[3]

Secondly, Henry needed ordination if he was to be settled as a pastor in Chester. This raised issues that went beyond doctrinal ones, for he had to decide whether he would submit to episcopal ordination, or else seek ordination at the hand of some Presbyterian ministers. A friend suggested to him that he could be ordained episcopally without the typical oaths and declarations to which the Puritans in general objected. He did not dismiss the matter summarily. He posed the question for himself: 'Whether it be *advisable* for one who hath devoted himself to the work of the ministry, but is by no means satisfied with the terms of conformity, to choose ordination by episcopal hands ... rather than ordination by presbyters, as some time practised by those of that persuasion?'

He had no doubt that episcopal ordination was lawful, particularly so in that the bishop could be considered as a presbyter acting along with his co-presbyters. Rather the issue was whether it was *advisable*. Not only did he think through the issue, but he left a document setting out his reasoning for rejecting episcopal ordination.[4] He noted that episcopal ordination was the law of the land, and Presbyterians never re-ordained someone who had received ordination by a bishop. Also, if the Act of Uniformity was ever revoked, then episcopal ordination might render a minister acceptable when Presbyterian ordination would disqualify him. On the other hand, Matthew Henry had reservations about the ordination of two distinct orders, deacons and priests. In the New Testament the deacons

---

3   Ibid, pp. 76-7.

4   The text is given in Tong, *Life of Matthew Henry*, pp. 76-81, and in Williams, *Memoirs*, pp. 44-7.

waited on tables, unlike the ministers who gave themselves to the Word and prayer. While recognising that the day might yet come when Presbyterian ordination would debar him from ministry, he preferred, if need be, to suffer for two truths:

1. That ordination by presbyters is (though not the only valid) yet the best, most scripturally regular, and therefore, the most eligible ordination.

2. That Jesus Christ never meant to make any of his ministers really priests, sacerdotes, otherwise than spiritual priests, as all believers are; nor that he ever meant to necessitate all his ministers to be deacons, that is, but overseers of the poor, or at best but half ministers at the first.

He ended his document with the words: 'Mine eyes are ever towards the Lord; shew me thy way, O Lord, and lead me in a plain path, because of my observers.' It was dated 28 April 1687.

Without any delay he proceeded to apply to leading Presbyterian ministers to whom he was already well known. But prior to this he had already examined his own heart and life in reference to the ministry. He prepared a document based on the words of 1 Timothy 4:15, 'Give thyself wholly to them.' It is unclear whether this was prepared as a sermon or simply as an exercise setting out his own understanding of the work of the ministry and the task to which he was setting himself. The title of the document is 'Serious Self-Examination before Ordination', and the opening statement is: 'That it is very requisite for a Man to examine himself very seriously at such a time, will readily be granted by those that consider the Nature of the ordinance, and of that Work into which it is a solemn entrance.' He posed six questions: What am I? What have I done? From what principles do I act in this undertaking? What are the ends that I aim at in this great undertaking? What do I want? What are my purposes and resolutions for the future?[5]

---

5   The full text is given in Tong, *Life of Matthew Henry*, pp. 57-73, and Williams, *Memoirs*, pp. 34-44.

The document shows how deeply he had thought about the steps he was just about to take towards ordination. He had examined his own heart in relation to his relationship with Christ, being convinced that he had accepted Christ on gospel terms to be his Prince to rule him and his Saviour to save him. He makes the declaration that, if God should ever call him to have charge over a flock, then he resolves to lay himself out for the spiritual good for his parishioners, and to be an example to them. In all the work ahead of him he pledged that he would 'esteem not only the crown of Christ, but the reproach of Christ, greater riches than the treasures of Egypt, having respect to the recompence of reward'.

The full extent of the examination for ordination is not clear, though he had to write a thesis in Latin on the subject, 'Are men justified by faith without the works of the law?' which was answered in the affirmative.[6] It was a short explanation of terms such as 'justified' and 'justified by faith' before setting out in brief the New Testament teaching that if justification was by the works of the law, then Christ had died in vain (Gal. 2:21).

The examining ministers set work for him to do, and he had to prepare a confession of his faith.[7] This he did under nine points, and in many places he summarised using words adapted from the Westminster Shorter Catechism. He used the accepted dual covenant pattern, a covenant of works 'promising life, upon condition of perfect obedience, threatening death upon disobedience', and a covenant of grace, 'made and published in the gospel, the tenor of which is, that all those who in the sight and sense of their lost and undone condition by nature come to Jesus Christ, and truly repent of all their sins, and heartily renounce the devil, the world, and the flesh ... have all their sins pardoned, their peace made, their persons justified, their natures sanctified, and their souls and bodies eternally saved'.

---

6   The Latin text is provided in Tong, *Life of Matthew Henry*, pp. 82-5.

7   The text is given both in Tong, ibid., pp. 85-91, and Williams, *Memoirs*, pp. 48-51.

A comparison of his wording on effectual calling with the Shorter Catechism shows his dependence on it (the words in italics are almost taken over verbatim):

S. C. Ques. 31 What is effectual calling?

Effectual calling is *a work of God's Spirit,* whereby, *convincing* us of our *sins* and misery, *enlightening* our *minds in the knowledge of Christ,* and *renewing* our *wills,* he doth *persuade and enable* us *to embrace Jesus Christ, freely offered* to us *in the gospel.*

The main change is that while the Shorter Catechism answer is given in the first person plural ('our sin', 'our minds', 'our wills', 'enable us', 'offered to us'), Matthew Henry phrases his statement in the third person plural ('working in them', 'convincing them', 'their minds', 'their wills', 'enabling them').

This point regarding his dependence on the wording of the Westminster divines is important, because it has been suggested that Matthew Henry was a more moderate Presbyterian than his father Philip Henry.[8] Whatever may have been true later, it is quite apparent that at the time of his ordination he was able to state his own doctrinal convictions in Westminster terms. This in turn suggests that he was standing on the same confessional base as his father Philip, and hence adopted no different doctrinal stance.

On 9 May 1687, Matthew Henry was duly ordained to the gospel ministry in London by six Presbyterian ministers. Because of the difficult religious and political times, it was considered appropriate to have the ordination in private, and the ministers gave him a very guarded certificate. It read:

We, whose names are subscribed, are well assured that Mr Matthew Henry is an ordained minister of the gospel.

---

8   See especially David P. Field, *Rigide Calvinisme in a Softer Dresse: The Moderate Presbyterianism of John Howe, 1630-1705* (Rutherford Studies in Historical Theology: Edinburgh: Rutherford House, 2004), pp.173-4. Field acknowledges that the contrast between Philip Henry's confession of 1657 with that of his son in 1687 'ought not to be overplayed'.

> Sic testor [so testified]
> W. Wickens
> Fran. Tallents.
> Edw. Lawrence.
> Nath. Vincent.
> James Owen.
> Rich. Steele.

May 9th, 1687[9]

Later Matthew Henry thought it best to have a fuller statement prepared regarding his ordination. He was in touch with two of the surviving ministers who took part in his ordination, Francis Tallents and James Owen, and they prepared the following statement:[10]

We, whose names are subscribed, being two of those six who subscribed a Certificate concerning the Ordination of Mr Matthew Henry, May 9. 1687, do hereby certifie, That the said certificate was drawn up short and general, because of the Difficulty of the Times, but the true interest and meaning of it was, that the said Mr Matthew Henry, after due Examination and Exercises performed with their Approbation, did upon the said 9th May 1687, at London, make a full Confession of his Faith, and Solemn Dedication of himself to the Service of Christ in the work of the ministry, and was thereupon, by Imposition of Hands, with Fasting and Prayer, ordained and set apart to the Work and Office of a Gospel Minister, by those whose Names are subscribed with their own Hands to the said Certificate.

> Fran. Tallents
> James Owen.

December 17, 1702.

---

9   Williams, *Memoirs*, p. 51, gives the date as 9 March 1687, but this is an obvious mistake. Matthew Henry's statement regarding episcopal ordination was made on 28 April 1687, and his ordination has to post-date it.

10   Tong, *Life of Matthew Henry*, pp. 91-2, and Williams, *Memoirs*, p. 271.

The ordination took place in the home of Mr Steel, with Mr Wickens presiding. Matthew Henry, writing about it in 1710, noted that 'Mr Steel preach'd and many Prayers were put up for me, which I trust I have far'd the better for. I then made my Ordination vows particularly, which are still a bond upon my soul. It was a Day never to be forgotten'.[11]

His father wrote him a letter soon after his ordination. In it he said:

> I rejoyce in what you heard and felt & saw of God on Munday last, & hope it hath left upon you a truly indelible character & such impressions as no time nor any thing else shall be able to wear out. Remember, Assisted by thy strength, ô God I wil— As to the manner & circumstances of your return, wee cannot order them here but must leave it to yoursf. to doe, as you shal see cause, beseeching the Lord in every th.[ing] to make your way playn before you, but as to the th.[ing] itsf. [itself] wee rejoyce in hopes, it wil not bee long now, ere wee shall see you here.[12]

An interesting reference follows in the letter to the fact that Katharine Henry had reservations about the call to Chester. Philip Henry said that he had often been swayed by his wife's opinions, but in this matter he left it till his son came to hear from his mother himself.

By 28 May, Matthew Henry was back down at his parents' home at Broad Oak, and his sister Sarah recorded her joy that her 'dear brother safe come home'. She also noted that the following day being the Sabbath, she and others of the family went to Whitewell Chapel to hear him preach, and in the evening he spoke on God's sparing mercy.

The continuing interest of the people in Chester in having him as their pastor was confirmed by the letters he received while still in London, and also by a personal visit from Mr

---

11 Roberts, *Matthew Henry and His Chapel*, p. 78.

12 Lee, *Diaries and Letters of Philip Henry*, p. 357.

Henthorn. Matthew Henry wrote that 'Mr Greg ply'd me with Letters, in many of which Mr Henthorn and others joyn'd, earnestly pressing me to persevere in my Intentions to come to Chester, and assuring me that upon their Application to Mr Harvy he had consented to my coming'.[13] The dissenting worshippers in Chester arranged for his friend William Tong to carry on ministry among them for several months until Matthew Henry could be settled as their pastor.

It was not surprising, therefore, that on 1 June 1687 a deputation from Chester, including Mr Greg, Mr Coker and Mr Hall, went to Broad Oak and accompanied him back to Chester. They had already arranged that Thursday would be the lecture day, and after personal conversation with Mr Harvey that assured him of his consent to his coming, Matthew Henry preached his first sermon on Thursday 2 June, on the text, 'I am determined to know nothing among you, but Jesus Christ, and him crucified' (1 Cor. 2:2). William Tong was present and he wrote: 'I am a Witness of the Joy and Thankfulness with which they received him; it may be truly said, they received him as an Angel of God.'[14]

---

13   Roberts, *Matthew Henry and His Chapel*, p. 77.

14   Tong, *Life of Matthew Henry*, p. 97.

CHAPTER 7

Early Ministry in Chester

It is fortunate that in addition to other sources of information about Matthew Henry's ministry in Chester we have his own account, the first part written in 1710 and the second part in 1712.[1] In the difficult years for the dissenters in Chester, Rev. John Harvey had ministered privately in his own house and elsewhere and managed to survive the years of persecution. He had been ordained in London by Bishop Worth in 1660, and ejected from the parish of Wallasey in Wirral in 1662. At the end of 1686 Matthew Henry preached at Mr Harvey's. With the change in the political climate and the expectation that the King would grant an indulgence to the dissenters, the dissenters in Chester started to meet openly. In addition to Mr Harvey's congregation, another group was ministered to by Rev. William Tong, who as we have already seen was a close friend of Matthew Henry and also his first biographer. As soon as Matthew Henry came to Chester, his friend moved to Wrexham and established a strong congregation there.

---

1   'A Short Account of the Beginning and Progress of Our Congregation by Mr Matthew Henry', Roberts, *Matthew Henry and His Chapel*, pp. 72-101.

A few Sundays before Matthew Henry arrived in Chester, the congregation that had been meeting in Mr Henthorn's hall moved to a large stable adjoining his house. Some alterations were quickly made at the congregation's expense and, as Matthew Henry noted, 'it was fitted up and made tolerably decent and convenient for the purpose'.[2] Later the congregation moved to the White-Friars, and worshipped there for thirteen years until land was purchased and a new chapel opened in August 1700.

As soon as his ministry commenced in Chester, he made it plain that his purpose was to expound the Scriptures in regular order. On the first Sunday he expounded Nehemiah 8, that relates how, on the return of the Jews from exile, Ezra and his companions 'read from the Book of the Law of God, making it clear and giving the meaning so that the people could understand what was being read' (Neh. 8:8). He announced to his congregation his intention to follow this example, and started the next Lord's Day with the book of Joshua. Soon he switched to Genesis and then dealt with the whole of the Old Testament in a period of about twenty years. By 1710 he was working through it again and had reached Numbers 10. He noted that he only dealt once with 'some parts not so edifying, on Sacrament Daies I expounded over the Gospel Psalms'.[3]

Here is a description of a normal Sunday for him:

> His constant work, on the Lord's Day, at Chester, was to pray six times in public, to sing six times, to expound twice and preach twice. He went to the congregation exactly at nine, began the public worship with singing the hundredth psalm; then prayed a short but fervent and suitable prayer, then he read some part of the Old Testament, and expounded it, going through it in course, from beginning to end; then he sang another psalm, then he prayed for about half an hour, then he preached and gave the blessing. He did the same exactly in the

---

2   Ibid., p. 79.

3   Ibid.

afternoon, only expounding the New Testament. This was his constant Lord's Day work.[4]

At first Matthew Henry did not have all his library with him, for it was still at his parents' home at Broad Oak. When writing to him on 28 November 1688, his father expressed his disappointment that he had not been able to get more of the books to him because of his horse's weakness and the 'fowlness' of the way to Chester. However, he gave him some good advice: 'You must digest those you have the better; esp. the Book of Bookes; Study that most & your own heart & the people's circumstances, & that wil doe much.'[5]

Matthew must have been very aware himself of advice his father regularly gave to prospective pastors. Students who had gone through their studies at private academies wanted to spend some time with Philip Henry and his family before they entered into the ministry. When they came to stay, what he did was to impress on them the need above all else to be familiar with the text of the Bible. He reminded them of the maxim, *bonus textarius est bonus theologus*, 'the good textual student is a good theologian'. He advised them to study Hebrew (they would have been already familiar with Greek and Latin), and to use an interleaved Bible in which they could insert observations they came across in sermons and other books. When the young men arrived at his home he became their counsellor:

> You come to me [he said] as Naaman did to Elisha expecting that I should do this & t'other for you, and alas! I can but say as he did 'Go wash in Jordan' Go, study the Scriptures. I profess to teach no other Learning but Scripture Learning. It was but a little before he died that in reading Isa.[iah] 50. he observed from *v.* 4. 'The Lord God hath given me the Tongue of the Learned' &c., that the true Learning of the Gospel

4   David Bogue and James Bennett, *History of Dissenters from the Revolution in 1688, to the year 1808* (London: Williams and Smith, 1808-1812), p. 361.

5   Lee, *Diaries and Letters of Philip Henry*, p. 361.

> Minister consists not in being able to speak Latin fluently, and to dispute in Philosophy, but in being able to speak a Word in Season to weary Souls. He that knows to do that well is a Learned Minister.[6]

The son gave good evidence from the outset of his ministry that he had listened well to his father's advice. His diary shows how assiduously he applied himself to his task as a pastor, noting what visits he had made, how often he preached and from what texts, the books he read, and his own spiritual state. Later, in a diary entry in the evening of the Lord's Day, 9 November 1696, he noted that he had finished preaching on 'redeeming the time' (Eph. 5.16). He had pointed out to his congregation that it was very useful 'to keep a short Account every night how the Day has been spent'. The purpose of this was to 'discover what are the Thieves of our Time, and will shew us what Progress we make in Holiness'. His advice to others was also meant to be taken seriously himself, and so he made this entry: 'And why now should I not make the experiment?'[7]

At first the congregation met at the same time as the parish church in the morning, but in the afternoon it met after the second service. This enabled Matthew Henry and others to attend the parish service, trying in this way to improve the relationship with the established church. However, this did not achieve its aim. Mr Greg, the leading layman in the congregation, pled with Dr Fog, the parish minister, that a softer attitude should be taken to them because of this attendance at the parish church. However, 'the Dr told him it made the matter no better. It was schismatical at any time'.[8] This caused the dissenters to review their practice, and Matthew Henry and his congregation soon started to worship morning and afternoon at the same time as the parish churches. Mr Harvey, who had

---

6   Ibid., pp. 333-4.

7   Tong, *Life of Matthew Henry*, pp. 110-11.

8   Roberts, *Matthew Henry and His Chapel*, p. 80.

had his meeting on the evening of the Lord's Day, soon followed the practice of the other congregation.

Not only was Matthew Henry occupied with the affairs of his own congregation, but he also attended Mr Harvey's lecture on Tuesday afternoons, and also that in St Michael's parish church as long as Dr Hancock remained the rector there. When he started to preach in the afternoon at church time on the Lord's Day in September 1687, he expounded Psalm 118 during the winter. From the spring of 1688 he commenced on the New Testament, and by 1710 he had almost finished doing so for a second time.

On the second Saturday he was in Chester, he started to catechise the children on Saturday afternoon. He heard them repeat answers from the Shorter Catechism, and expounded them one at a time. When his own catechism was published, he examined them on that.[9] The choice of Saturday afternoon was that it gave him greater time and freedom with the children than if he had to do it on the Lord's Day. In alternate years when he had finished the catechism, he preached a special sermon for the children at their usual meeting time. No record remains of these sermons, but presumably they were adapted to suit the needs of the children.

During the winter of 1689 Matthew Henry set up a private conference to consider a theological topic, and this practice continued right throughout his ministry. It was, as he wrote in 1712, 'manag'd with all the seriousness, and yet with all the agreeable freedom we could; the Question was propos'd before, which each spoke to at our coming together, and I sum'd up all at last, and we began and concluded with Prayer'.[10] His eldest and favourite sister, Sarah (Mrs Savage), recorded in her diary an occasion in 1697 when she was present at a conference. The subject she heard discussed was the benefits flowing from

---

9   *A Scripture Catechism*, in *The Complete Works*, vol. II, pp. 174-258.

10   'A Short Account of the Beginning and Progress of Our Congregation by Mr Matthew Henry,' Roberts, *Matthew Henry and His Chapel*, p. 88.

justification, adoption and sanctification, according to the Westminster Shorter Catechism.[11]

Shortly after going to Chester, Matthew Henry went to see Mr Harvey again. On this occasion he proposed that the two congregations should be united and that he become the assistant to his senior brother, or at least that they celebrate the Lord's Supper together. Mr Harvey rejected the offer or, as Matthew Henry himself put it, 'he peremptorily refused both, saying we would each stand on our own bottom'.[12] This left the way clear for Matthew Henry to go ahead and administer the Lord's Supper to his own congregation, which he did on the second Sunday in July, 1687. About forty-five who had previously been communicants in the congregations ministered to by Mr Cook and Mr Hall partook of the Lord's Supper, together with ten young men who were new communicants. After that, communion was observed on the first Sunday of the month. Very quickly the blessing on Matthew Henry's ministry was seen in that there were often ten or twelve or fifteen new communicants every month. Within two to three years his congregation consisted of about 250 communicants, and the services, especially the afternoon ones, were thronged.

For some years from 1690 onwards a national public fast was authorised on the second Wednesday of every month from April till November. Matthew Henry observed these very solemnly. He preached at them and also very large offerings were taken up. This money was used initially for the poor from Ireland who had crossed over to England. Even when the national fast days were no longer stipulated, Matthew Henry's congregation kept them. Sometimes he was helped by another minister such as Mr Jonathan Harvey, Mr Lea and Mr Robert Murrey. Offerings were taken and these went to pay the rent and do repairs on their building in which they worshipped, to help their own poor, and to answer all 'briefs' brought to them.

---

11   Ibid., p. 89 fn.

12   Ibid., p. 81.

These 'briefs' were voluntary collections for various sufferers, but for the Chester area they were mainly for the work of the established churches, not for dissenting chapels that were vandalised or burned to the ground.

The early part of his ministry took place during the final period of the reign of James II. When the King came to Chester in September 1687, both Mr Harvey and Matthew Henry presented addresses of thanks to the King for the fact that they were now living in peace and liberty under his protection. When the Glorious Revolution took place at the end of 1688, many dissenters had to flee from Ireland. While the ministers went to London, the people stayed in towns like Chester, and Matthew Henry's congregation was greatly enlarged by their numbers. However, following the Battle of the Boyne in July 1690, many of these returned to Ireland.

Late in 1689 Matthew Henry wrote the first of his many publications. He discussed the whole question of schism in a thirty-four page pamphlet entitled 'A Brief Enquiry into the True Nature of Schism: or A Persuasive to Christian Love and Charity'.[13] It was a difficult period for the dissenters, for although they now had formal freedom of worship yet often local feeling spilled over into opposition and even persecution. Clearly he was attempting to answer some of the objections to the dissenting ministers and their congregations being presented by people in the established church. He addressed the question of how differences of opinion could be managed within the one body, and if it could not, how the dissenters could follow their consciences in setting up separate assemblies for worship. He called this 'a lawful and justifiable separation, (though I would rather call it a diversity of communion, from the parish churches)'.[14] This was not a setting up of altar against altar, but altar by altar. It was unity of love and commitment to Christ he sought, rather than 'uniformity in modes and ceremonies'.

---

13   The text can be found in *The Complete Works*, vol. II, pp. 353-61.

14   Ibid., p. 359.

The pamphlet was published at the urging of Matthew Henry's friend William Tong, though it did not carry Matthew Henry's name as author. It certainly caused a stir, because a writer who called himself 'T. W. a citizen of Chester' answered in another pamphlet. Matthew Henry, who did not like 'law wars, nor sword wars, nor book wars', decided not to answer, but William Tong took up the cudgels on his behalf. It would have been better if William Tong had let the matter die, for another anonymous publication came out. Matthew Henry's comment on it, in a letter to his father was:

> We were surprised the other night, with a 'review' of the new notion of schism and the vindicator of it—by an unknown hand; superior to T. W. in learning and reading; but a very little inferior in spleen and bitterness, and unfairness. When I speak they are for war; and who can help it?[15]

Such pamphlet warfare was typical of the era, whereas in more modern times other media would have been used to propagate views. This was the only time that Matthew Henry published anything anonymously.[16]

The early period of his ministry in Chester was also marked by notable events in his personal and family life. He had already heard about Katharine Hardware, and on going to Chester desired to marry her. However, Mrs Hardware was not at all willing for this to happen, and considered a dissenting pastor did not have enough of this world's goods to care for her daughter, who had already received proposals from gentlemen with much larger estates. She was also worried that the liberty the dissenters presently enjoyed was precarious, and was concerned how her daughter would cope if persecution arose again. 'She question'd', as William Tong described it, 'whether

---

15 Williams, *Memoirs*, p. 223. The last sentence is an allusion to Ps. 120:7: 'I am a man of peace; but when I speak, they are for war'.

16 For further discussion of this pamphlet, along with his other writings, see pp. 173-5.

her Daughter would have Faith and Patience enough to encounter with it, having been tenderly brought up, and every where treated with Respect and Honour, and if she could not stoop to the Cross, she considered it would be a great addition to Mr Henry's Troubles in a Time when he would have most need of Comfort'.[17] Later Mrs Hardware admitted that she had been governed by 'covetousness and pride' when she tried to prevent the marriage. In the end true love prevailed, the marriage taking place in July 1687. For four months the young couple stayed in the house of Mr Greg, one of the prominent members of the congregation, and then moved in October to premises in the Friary that had been occupied by Mr Harvey. This was to be home for Matthew Henry for the next twenty-two years. It should be added that Katharine's mother regretted her initial stand about the marriage, but recognised that God had overruled for good.

Philip Henry gave excellent advice to his son and new daughter-in-law by penning some poetry for them. This was advice 'from a pious aged father to his son a minister newly married'.

> Dear Pair, whom God hath now of two made One
> Suffer a Father's exhortation.
> In the first Place see that with joynt indeavor—
> You set yourselves to serve the Lord together,
> You are yoakt to work but for work Wages write,
> His Yoak is easie, & his burden light,
> Love one another, Pray oft together, and see,
> You never both together Angry bee—
> If one speak fire t'other with water come,
> Is one provok'd be tother soft or dumb—
> Walk low, but aim high, spotless be your life
> You are a Minister, and a Minister's Wife
> Therefore as Beacons set upon a Hill—
> To angels and to men a spectacle—

---

17 Tong, *Life of Matthew Henry*, p. 103.

Your slips will falls be calld, your falls each one
Will be a blemish to Religion—
Do good to all, bee affable and meek
Your converse must be Preaching all the week—
Your Garb and Dress must not be vain or Gay,
Reckon good works your richest, best array—
Your House must be a Bethel, and your Door
Always stand open to relieve the Poor
Call your estate God's, not your own, ingrave
Holiness to the Lord on all you have
Count upon suffering, or you count amis,
Sufficient to each day its evil is,
All are born once to trouble, but saints twice,
And as experience shews Min[iste]rs thrice,
But if you suffer with and for your Lord,
You'l reign with him according to his Word.[18]

The marriage was an extremely happy one, but only lasted eighteen months. Katharine contracted smallpox and died on 14 February 1689 after giving birth to a daughter. She was only twenty-five years of age. Katharine's mother bore the tragedy well and acknowledged that it was the Lord's will. His friend William Tong came to console Matthew who, after shedding tears, was able to say: 'I know nothing that could support me under such a loss as this, but the good hope that she is gone to heaven, and that, in a little time, I shall follow her thither.' She was buried in Trinity Church, Chester[19] on Saturday, 16 February 1689, with a service at Matthew Henry's chapel afterwards, when Mr Lawrence preached on Philippians 1:21: 'To die is gain.'

---

18 Lee, *Diaries and Letters of Philip Henry*, pp. 359-60.

19 None of the sources explain how a dissenting minister's wife could be buried 'within the altar' of a Church of England, in a tomb where Matthew Henry's body was later interred. The warm relationships that both Philip and Matthew Henry had with Anglican clergymen may well explain the offer of this burial place. A small brass plate was placed 'under the creed' noting the particulars of Katharine Henry, and later those concerning Matthew Henry were added. For the Latin text (and English translation), see Williams, *Memoirs*, p. 272.

Philip Henry came to console his son, whose grief was tempered by the fact that the life of his first-born was spared. She was called Katharine after her mother, and baptised by her grandfather. Her father made the usual confession of faith in Christ, but then added:

> Although my house be not now so with God, yet he hath made with me an everlasting covenant, ordered in all things and sure, and this is all my salvation, and all my desire, although he make me not to grow; and according to the tenor of this covenant, I offer up this child to the Great God, a plant out of a dry ground, desiring that it may be implanted into Christ.[20]

The large congregation present was deeply touched by this, and burst into tears.

Matthew Henry continued on with his normal ministerial work, and also continued to live with his deceased wife's parents. After some time Mrs Hardware recommended that he marry again, and even suggested a relative of her own, Mary Warburton. She had godly parents. Her father and grandfather were both devout Christian men. In his later years her father spent much of his time in reading and prayer, and his Bible and a copy of Richard Baxter's *The Saints' Everlasting Rest*, were always on the parlour table. Her mother was a Londoner, and shared both her husband's faith and his commitment to the nonconformist cause. Ejected ministers, who were silenced by their expulsion from their parishes, found a ready welcome at the Warburton home, and dissenting believers often gathered there.

The wedding took place on 8 July 1690 at the bride's home at Grange in Cheshire. The Henrys senior were present, and a few days later accompanied their son and their new daughter-in-law to Chester. When they had settled in, the Hardwares left Chester and went back to live in their own estate at

---

20   Williams, *Memoirs*, p. 57.

Bromborough Court in Wirral. Matthew and Mary were blessed by the arrival of a daughter, Elizabeth, on 12 April 1691 who was baptised by her grandfather Philip on the normal lecture day in his son's congregation.

The household joy was not to last long, for Elizabeth took ill when about three months old. She had whooping cough and a fever. From 9 November 1690 Matthew Henry had kept a diary, and so we can read his reaction to this illness. Just three days before Elizabeth died, he wrote:

> The child has been ill all night; she is very weak, and in all appearance worse; but I am much comforted by her baptism. I desire to leave her in the arms of him who gave her to me. The will of the Lord be done. I have said, if the Lord will spare her, I will endeavour to bring her up for *him*. I am now sitting by her, thinking of the mischievous nature of original sin, by which death reigns over poor infants.

On the day of her death he penned these words:

> In the morning I had the child in my arms, endeavouring solemnly to give her up to God, and to bring my heart to his will: and presently there seemed some reviving. But while I was writing this, I was suddenly called out of my closet. I went for the doctor, and brought him with me; but, as soon as we came in, the sweet babe quietly departed between the mother's arms and mine, without any struggle, for nature was spent by its long illness; and now my house is a house of mourning.

He endeavoured to comfort his wife as they prepared for the funeral. When it was over he wrote: 'I have been this Day doing a Work that I never did, burying a Child, a sad Day's Work.' Friends came and showed their kindness to the bereaved family, and attended the afternoon lecture at which his good friend Mr Lawrence preached from Psalm 39:9: 'I was dumb, I opened not my mouth, because thou didest it.'

Another daughter, Mary, was born two years later, on 3 April 1693. The grandfather came from Broad Oak and baptised both her and her cousin, Katherine Hulton, and in his diary he records the prayer: 'The Lord write their Names in the Book of the Living.'[21] But this baby only lived three weeks, dying the same month on 22 April. In Matthew Henry's diary he expressed his grief, and then wrote: 'The Lord is righteous, he takes and gives, gives and takes again; I desire to submit, but, O Lord, shew me wherefore thou contendest with me.'[22] On the following Lord's Day he expounded Job 38, a passage dealing with the assertion of God's sovereignty, while he preached on Romans 5:14: 'Nevertheless Death reigned from Adam to Moses, even over them that had not sinned, after the similitude of Adam's transgression, who is the figure of him who was to come.' Even when noting that within the year two of his children and two of his sisters had been buried in Trinity Church, he can still say: 'The Lord is gracious.'

Joy came to the Henrys in the following year when a daughter, Esther, was born on 27 September 1694. Despite various illnesses, especially one when she was three years old, she survived. At that time Matthew Henry referred to her as 'the Delight of my Eyes'.

---

21   Tong, *Life of Matthew Henry*, p. 116.

22   Williams, *Memoirs*, p. 61.

CHAPTER 8

Later Ministry at Chester (to 1710)

The work begun in Chester in 1686 was carried on without much variation for the next twenty-six years. Each Lord's Day he continued to have the two services, expounding the Old Testament in the morning and the New Testament in the afternoon, as well as preaching a sermon at both. He would often pray for half an hour, and at times would use the Lord's Prayer. While others refused to use it, Matthew Henry did, and was ready to defend his action. He noted in his diary that he was being criticised for this and on one occasion he penned these words: 'I wrote to Mr Farrington, why he should not be offended at my using the Lord's prayer.'[1]

He commenced his morning service with the singing of Psalm 100. A psalm was sung after his exposition and before he preached. At the end of the service another psalm, often the 117th, was sung before the benediction. These singings were *a cappella*, as no musical instrument was used in dissenting services at that period. In 1694 Matthew Henry published a volume entitled, *Family Hymns, Gathered Mostly out of the Translations of David's Psalms.*[2] He preferred singing songs taken from Scripture, though in the third edition he included paraphrases of passages from Isaiah, Luke 1–2, the book of Revelation, and Ambrose's *Te Deum* ('We praise Thee, O God; we acknowledge Thee to be the Lord'). Also, to some other

---

1 Williams, *Memoirs*, p. 112.

2 It is included in *The Complete Works*, Vol. I, pp. 413-43.

selections he added a New Testament doxology, such as placing Revelation 5:12-13 after his setting of Psalm 110. He explained his action by saying that the inclusion of 'some of the New-Testament Hymns, which being calculated for gospel times, will, I doubt not, be very agreeable to every good Christian'.[3]

In a preface to the reader he indicated that his concern was to promote singing at family worship. He pointed out that it was the ancient practice of Christians to sing in the home, and he quotes from a variety of sources – from the New Testament, from writers such as Pliny, Clement of Alexandria, Tertullian and Cyprian and on to those of more recent times in England. According to him, it did not matter if neighbours heard the singing as Christians serve a master of whom they have no reason to be ashamed. As to the manner of singing, he insisted that with only a small degree of skill a family could manage to sing the Psalms, and in families 'the quickest way of singing seems to be the most agreeable'.[4]

'Family Hymns' consists of ninety hymns, though often a hymn is made up of selections from several different psalms or biblical passages. Here is an example of one set out for the Lord's Day morning.

> HYMN XXVII   Ps. xxvii.4
> This is my great request, O God,
> Which here I do present,
> That all the days I have to live
> May in thy house be spent.
> There to contemplate and behold
> The beauty of the Lord,
> And in his temple to inquire
> Into his holy word.
>
> 8, 9
>
> When as thou saidst, My face seek ye,
> Instructed by thy grace,

---

3   Ibid., p. 415.

4   Ibid., p. 414.

My ready heart with joy replied,
Lord, I will seek thy face.
Hide not thy face from me in wrath;
Lord turn me not away:
My Saviour, thou hast been my help,
Be still my strength and stay.

_____xliii. 3, 4

O send out light and truth divine,
To lead and bring me near
Unto that holy hill of thine,
And tabernacles there.
Then to God's altar I will go,
The gladness of my joy,
O God, my God, thy praise to show,
My harp I will employ.

_____cxix.32

And I will run with full consent
The way thou givest in charge,
When with thy sweet encouragement
Thou shalt my heart enlarge.

No music was printed, but sometimes a note was given indicating that the psalm was to be sung to the tune of Psalm 67, or that the hymns of praise (comprising Hymns 67 to 90) were to be sung to the tune of the 100th Psalm and the 148th Psalm. This means that the first section of this group were Long Metre (and could be sung to the tune The Old 100th), while the later ones were in 6.6.6.6.8.8 metre. One practice that Matthew Henry sought to discourage was giving out each line before it was sung. This was an English custom to enable those who could not read to join in the singing. This practice of 'lining-out' meant that the singing took much longer, and in general resulted in a very slow pace. In the discussions at the Westminster Assembly, the Scottish commissioners argued against the practice, but *The Directory of Public Worship* included reference to it.[5] What Matthew Henry suggested was that each member of the family have a book so that the psalm or hymn:

> may be sung without reading the line betwixt, which is the general practice of the reformed churches abroad, and renders the duty more pleasant and profitable, and takes up less time, and is practicable enough in a family, if not in large congregations.[6]

Acknowledgment was given that the work of others had been used. This included the translations by Patrick, Barton, Bishop King, Smith, Dr Ford and Baxter. The best were taken and as it suited his purpose, for he acted, he wrote, 'not as a censor, but as a gleaner'. He hoped this general acknowledgment would free him from any charge of plagiarism. His ultimate aim was beautifully expressed in the closing sentences of the preface:

> The performance indeed is but very small, yet the design is honest; and it will be fruit abounding to a good account, if it do but help forward the work of singing psalms in which the will of God is done on earth, somewhat like it is in heaven, where singing hallelujahs to him that sits upon the throne, and unto the Lamb, is both the everlasting work, and the everlasting felicity, of those glorified beings that wear the crown of perfection within the vail.[7]

The translation of the biblical passages shows not only borrowing from others, but also Matthew Henry's own judgment on the

---

5   As a result of the influence of *The Directory of Public Worship* the practice of lining-out was adopted in Scotland, and 'when in 1746 the General Assembly [of the Church of Scotland] recommended its discontinuance there were angry protests against the interference with an 'old Scottish custom', though in fact it was less than a century old' (W. Lamb, *The Psalms in Christian Worship* [London: The Faith Press, 1962], p. 158). The practice continues till the present wherever Scottish Gaelic is used, and also in some Afro-American congregations in the U.S.A., especially at communion services.

6   *The Complete Works*, vol. I, p. 414.

7   Ibid, pp. 414-15.

meaning of the Hebrew text. For example, he departs from the common rendering of the last verse of Psalm 23. The Authorised Version has: 'Surely goodness and mercy shall follow me all the days of my life, and I shall dwell in the house of the Lord for ever,' while the Scottish metrical version renders it by the words:

Goodness and mercy all my life,
Shall surely follow me,
And in God's house forevermore
My dwelling place shall be.

The Hebrew text simply finishes the psalm with the words, 'and I shall return to the house of the LORD for length of days'. This suggests that David was thinking about constantly returning to the tabernacle, rather than contemplation of a heavenly abode. Matthew Henry picks this up with his metrical translation:

Surely thy goodness and thy grace
Shall always follow me;
And my perpetual dwelling place
Thy holy house shall be.

While the translations are very close to the Hebrew text, at times there is interpretation that intrudes a distinctly New Testament idea into the text. Thus, for example, in Psalm 51, after very accurate translation of the opening verses, verse 7 is given in this form:

With hyssop sprinkle me, and then
shall be clean, I know;
And make me with my Saviour's blood
Whiter than driven snow.

The linking of Old Testament and New Testament concepts became even more explicit when Matthew Henry concluded a rendering of Psalm 110 with a metrical paraphrase of Revelation 5:12-13.

Therefore to thee, O Lamb of God,
Riches and power belong,

Wisdom and honour, glory, strength,
And every praising song.
From every tongue and nation hast
Redeemed us unto God.
Blessing and honour, glory, power,
From all in earth and heaven,
To him that sits upon the throne,
And to the Lamb be given.[8]

In a similar way he concluded his setting of Psalm 95 with a paraphrase of Hebrews 4:1:

Let us then fear lest, a like rest
Being now proposed to us,
Any of us through unbelief
Come short and perish thus.

This combination was a perceptive use of the Hebrews passage to link Psalm 95 with its New Testament application. The author of Hebrews applied the psalmist's warning to those to whom he was writing.

In these respects he was moving in the way that Isaac Watts would do shortly afterwards, as he sought to bring out the Christian application of the Psalms. Matthew Henry continued to work on the family hymns, and in the middle of 1702 he brought out a second edition, 'with large additions'.[9]

His sermons were always meticulously prepared, written in a small hand on eight pages of paper. His language was clear and precise, but with turns of phrase that made his sayings memorable. Doubtless, to some extent his speech and writing was patterned after his father's, though there is much originality about it. In writing his father's life, he gave extended illustrations of his sayings, culled from letters, sermons and expositions.[10]

---

8   Ibid., p. 430.

9   For further discussion on Matthew Henry's hymns, see the helpful article by H. O. Old, 'Matthew Henry and the Puritan Discipline of Family Prayer', *Calvin Studies VII* (1994), pp. 72-6.

10   *The Life of the Rev. Philip Henry*, pp. 235-66.

Only one extended piece of Philip Henry's writing is extant, one copied by Matthew when he was about twenty years of age. This is his exposition of the first eleven chapters of the book of Genesis.[11] It is hardly surprising that the son patterned himself in speech and writing on his father. Matthew was not aiming at being conspicuously different from other preachers, but simply used pointed metaphors and unusual sayings to grip hold of the minds of his listeners and readers. A collection of his sayings drawn from his *Exposition* was published in 1781.[12]

Certainly he was fond of alliteration, and though he did not employ it all the time, on occasions it made memorisation of his main points very easy. Here is an example taken from a sermon dealing with the living God, a pardoning God. His headings were:

How *free* his pardons are.
How *full* his pardons are.
How *frequent* his pardons are.
How *firm* his pardons are.
How *forward* he is to pardon.
How *faithful* and just he is in pardoning.[13]

Another example comes from a sermon on the text, 'Peace I leave with you. My peace I give unto you, not as the world giveth, give I unto you' (John 14:27).

It is *satisfying* to all our desires.
It is *silencing* to all our fears.

---

11 Philip Henry, *An Exposition with Practical Observations, upon the First Eleven Chapters of the Book of Genesis* (London: J. Nisbet and Co., 1839). This book was from a manuscript in Matthew Henry's handwriting passed down to a descendant, John Lee of Whitchurch, Shropshire, who published it to elucidate some of the 'beautiful and excellencies of the sacred volume, that it may be made instrumental in promoting the glory of God, and in setting forth "the unsearchable riches of Christ",' p. viii.

12 *Select Sentences collected from the Rev. Mr Henry's Exposition of the Old and New Testament* (London: James Buckland, 1781).

13 *Unpublished Sermons on the Covenant of Grace*, pp. 53-6.

It is *securing* in all our dangers.

It is *solacing* in all our sorrows.

It is *sweetening* to all our comforts.[14]

Three discussions on Matthew Henry in the nineteenth century deal with his language. J. B. Williams, his biographer, admits that at times his colloquialisms may sometimes amuse, as do his antitheses, which are 'too frequent and jingling'. However, this language must be understood in the context of his aim to 'give the sense, and cause men to understand the reading'.[15] In the special annual lecture of the Presbyterian Church of England for 1879, A. B. Grosart dealt with the sanctified common sense of Matthew Henry, and in so doing drew attention to the wit and brevity of many of his sayings. His judgment was: 'It is the combination of wit with brevity and brevity with wit, that makes his Commentary such racy and delightful reading, and so memorable. You recognise that the man says something because he has got something to say.'[16] Similarly, John Stoughton commented on his language, a result of God's gift of 'a peculiar genius and a peculiar training, and the man cultivated that genius and improved that training'.[17] He was not aiming at being exceptional with his 'pointed metaphors and trite sayings'. Rather, he aimed at being useful as he adapted himself to the wants and needs of his time.[18]

Every month he dispensed the Lord's Supper in this congregation, and in all the years he was at Chester he only missed doing so once when he had smallpox. At the beginning and end of his Chester ministry he did not have any definite scheme for his preaching at the celebration of the Lord's Supper, but for fourteen years, from 1696 to 1710, he had a series on the suf-

14   Ibid., pp. 97-9.

15   Williams, *Memoirs*, pp. 250-4.

16   A. B. Grosart, *Representative Nonconformists: With the Message of Their Life-work for To-day* (London: Hodder and Stoughton, 1879), p. 314. He lists on pp. 315-42 some of Matthew Henry's memorable sayings in his *Exposition*.

17   John Stoughton, *Lights of the World; or, Illustrations of Character drawn from the Records of Christian Life*, 2nd ed (London: Religious Tract Society, n. d.)

18   Ibid., pp. 164-5.

ferings and death of Christ, followed by many sermons dealing with the spiritual state of those partaking of communion. Then he dealt with the penitent and pious reflections of communicants before he finished the series with forty-three sermons on the great promises to believers.[19]

On several occasions he returned to London. In May 1698 he travelled with his friend William Tong, preaching at various places on the way, including Nantwich, Lichfield and Sutton Coldfield. In the metropolis he preached practically every day of his visit. One particular sermon at a fast day in Mr John Howe's church on Acts 28:22 ('A sect every where spoken against'), was published, with some enlargement, the following year. Matthew Henry himself noted that he did so 'at the request of a very worthy friend who heard it preached in London last summer'.[20] It is most probable that the friend was William Tong, though he does not name him.

His wife accompanied him when he returned to London in 1704, though the reasons for their trip are not clear. They arrived in London on a Saturday and the following day they heard Rev. John Howe preaching on Jude 21. In his diary Matthew Henry recorded this comment: 'The text was Jude 21; and I must never forget what he said in the close of the sermon. "I would deal for your souls, as for my own, and for myself I declare before you all, I depend upon the mercy of our Lord Jesus Christ for eternal life".'[21]

For twenty years Henry also preached to prisoners in the castle at Chester. While many of them were there long-term because of debt, yet others were imprisoned for violent crimes and some were awaiting execution. At times not only were prisoners affected by his preaching, but others present were so touched that tears flowed freely. The gaoler's wife was the instrumental cause of him beginning

---

19 The list can be found in Tong, *Life of Matthew Henry,* pp. 197-207, and is reprinted in Williams, *Memoirs,* pp. 288-92.

20 See the preface to the sermon entitled 'Discourse concerning Meekness and Quietness of Spirit to which is added a Sermon Acts XXVIII.22', *The Complete Works,* vol. II, pp. 96-156.

21 Quoted in Williams, *Memoirs*, pp. 87-8.

this ministry. She was a religious woman, and had a deep concern for the prisoners, and especially noted that no preaching was provided for them. Because she treated them with tenderness and compassion, they were

Matthew Henry's chapel, Chester, built in 1700.

ready to listen to the preacher who came as a result of her pleadings. Matthew Henry went about once every three weeks, sometimes oftener, and preached to them on a week day. He also had a collection for them. On occasions he was called in specially to speak but after some time, due to administrative changes at the castle, he had to discontinue this practice.[22]

While the actual attendances at the various services in his congregation are unknown, yet the fact that his congregation grew until it had over 350 communicants testifies to the appreciation of his ministry. The first sign of the growth of the congregation was when another bay had to be added to the building they were using. Several reasons combined to convince Matthew Henry and his congregation that a new meeting house of their own was something for which they should aim. The building they were using had belonged to Mr Anthony Henthorn, but he left for Ireland in 1692, and his son Samuel died in 1695. His grandson John was not as favourably disposed to the dissenting congregation, or, as Matthew Henry himself put it, he 'did not countenance us as he [his grandfather] had done'.[23]

A piece of ground was purchased in Crook Street, Chester, and the foundation of the building was laid in September 1699.

---

22   Further information about his ministry to prisoners is given by Tong, *Life of Matthew Henry*, pp. 236-42, with some listing of the texts of Scripture he used on these occasions.

23   Roberts, *Matthew Henry and His Chapel*, p. 91.

The construction really got under way in February 1700, and the chapel was finished in July. The subscription list showed that 242 contributors gave a total of £491.10.03, while the building costs were given as £532.16.01, and the debt was soon cleared. Matthew Henry's own contribution of £20.00.00 was only bettered by one other giver. His brother-in-law, John Hulton, was responsible for the collection of the money and the payment of the accounts.[24] In August 1700 the congregation moved into its new building, after being thirteen years in the former premises. It was on a regular lecture day that Matthew Henry first preached in the new chapel, with his text being Joshua 22:22-23: 'The LORD God of gods, he knows if it be in rebellion or transgression against the LORD that we have built us an altar.'[25] His sister Sarah wrote about the first occasion when the Lord's Supper was administered in the new chapel.

> I had a comfortable day joining with that assembly in holy ordinances. In the forenoon, Brother went on in expounding gospel Psalms, such as especially look at Christ. To-day Psalm lxix. We had the Sacrament of the Lord's supper (the first in the new Chapel) administered.... He told us that much of religion lies in the eye of a believing soul being fixed on an all-seeing God. The subject was 2 Cor. xiii.5, *Examine yourselves whether ye be in the faith.*[26]

Matthew Henry's own comment (written in 1712) on the chapel was this: 'It is very commodious, capacious, pleasant place, and many a comfortable Day we have had in it. Blessed be God.'[27]

Various pictures of the chapel exist. It was built of stone with a triple gable, and, in typical dissenting style, resembled

---

24   The full list of subscriptions is given in Roberts, ibid., pp. 244-7, with the expenses of the building on pp. 247-8.

25   The sermon was not published at the time, but it was in 1726 with an introduction by Dr Isaac Watts.

26   Quoted in Roberts, *Matthew Henry and His Chapel*, p. 91.

27   Ibid., pp. 91-2.

domestic dwellings rather than traditional church buildings.[28] The interior was plain, with the pulpit on one of the long walls so that the seating could be arranged to give worshippers good vision of the minister leading the worship. All the pews were

The interior of Matthew Henry's chapel showing the gallery, built in 1707.

enclosed with wooden partitions, each having a door. The chapel existed until 1960, when it was demolished to make way for redevelopment in the centre of Chester.[29]

Further change to the congregation and its growth came through the death of Mr John Harvey. He died in November 1699, and his son Jonathan succeeded him, but he was not ordained until 1701. Prior to that date Mr Lea, of Wirral, celebrated the Lord's Supper for the congregation. At the request of some of Mr Harvey's congregation, Matthew Henry started to preach the preparatory sermon once a month for that con-

28 See the excellent discussion by Christopher Stell, 'Puritan and Nonconformist Meetinghouses in England', in Paul Corby Finney, ed., *Seeing beyond the Word: Visual Arts and the Calvinist Traditions* (Grand Rapids: Eerdmans, 1991), pp. 49-81.

29 The Unitarian congregation in possession of the chapel built a new chapel in Nevin Road, Blacon, and took some of the items from the old one. These included the pulpit, a baptismal font, a table, wooden panelling on the walls, and two stained-glass windows (of Matthew Henry and James Martineau). This congregation dwindled away and the chapel became derelict until purchased by an evangelical group in 1988, and today it is the Matthew Henry Evangelical Church.

gregation, and in return Mr Jonathan Harvey preached at the quarterly fast in the Crook Street chapel. He also did so at the lecture day if Matthew Henry was absent from Chester. Certainly it appears that a drift of members from Mr Harvey's congregation occurred, with quite a few making their way to the Crook Street chapel, for Matthew Henry recorded in his diary:

> I have had many searchings of heart about Mr Harvey's congregation who come dropping in on us. As I have endeavoured, in that matter, to approve myself to God, and my own conscience; and my heart doth not reproach me; so, blessed by God, I hear not of any person, one or others that doth.[30]

In September 1706 Mr Jonathan Harvey left Chester. His health was impaired and a dispute had taken place about the meeting place of his congregation. He told Matthew Henry that his congregation had failed to secure their meeting place and he was determined to leave. By late that month Matthew Henry noted in his diary that on the Lord's Day, 29 September, 'Mr Harvy's people with us & many strangers'. Later, he recorded that at the celebration of the Lord's Supper in November of that year twelve members of Mr Harvey's congregation had formally joined his congregation. By Christmas the greater part of the congregation had transferred their membership, though, wrote Matthew Henry in 1710, 'many of them with an express Protestation that if he [Mr Harvey] resumed the meeting they would return to him'.[31]

The increased size of the congregation necessitated some expansion of the Crook Street chapel, and so it was decided that a gallery would be built. The work started on 7 April 1707, cost £85 and subscriptions covered this amount.[32] By Matthew Henry's reckoning his congregation by that time had more than 350 communicants, with about 300 normally present. Though

---

30 This extract is given both in Williams, *Memoirs*, p. 136, and in Roberts, *Matthew Henry and His Chapel*, p. 92.

31 Roberts, ibid., p. 93.

32 Ibid., pp. 248-50 contain the list of subscribers for the building and the gallery, and also the disbursements to meet the costs.

he wrote that there was 'a great deal of comfort and unanimity among us, and my ministry well accepted', yet he had discouragements as well. At the end of 1707 he wrote in his diary:

> As to my ministry here, Mr Mainwaring's leaving me, and his wife has been very much my discouragement. But Providence ordered it that Mr Harvey's congregation are generally come in to us, or else we began to dwindle, so that I should have gone on very heavily.[33]

It is difficult to estimate accurately the numbers attending his congregation. If 300 communicants were present, then many others must have been attending also, including the children of the communicants. According to the statistics compiled by Dr John Evans between 1715 and 1718, the number of Presbyterian hearers in Chester numbered 1,000. For the whole of Cheshire in the early eighteenth century, eighteen Presbyterian congregations existed, with 8,000 hearers. This meant that out of a total population for Cheshire of 111,700, the Presbyterians accounted for 7.25%. By comparison, the General and Particular Baptists had only seven congregations with 330 hearers, this number being only 0.3% of the total population.[34]

Various other forms of discouragement came to him at Chester, some from the outside community, others from within the congregation. Feeling still ran high against the dissenters, in spite of the passing of the Toleration Act in 1689. For example, in 1694 arsonists tried to burn down Matthew Henry's chapel. From within the congregation he was discouraged when he sought to carry out any reproof or discipline. He investigated the facts in every case, and any reproof was intended to restore the offending person. Sometimes his approach to them was rejected, and instead they subjected him to personal attacks, denouncing him as uncharitable and severe. When this happened, it was, he wrote in his diary,

---

33   Diary for 31 December 1707, quoted in Williams, *Memoirs*, p. 93.

34   These figures are taken from Michael R. Watts, *The Dissenters from Reformation to the French Revolution* (Oxford: Clarendon Press, 1978), pp. 494 and 509.

a temptation to me to lay aside the pastoral charge, but I dare not. I cannot do it. My God will humble me. Let him that thinketh he standeth, or is thought by his friends to stand, take heed lest he fall. The Lord make it a warning to me and to us all.[35]

Some of those people left his congregation. Others, while not concurring altogether in the rules of discipline applied in the Crook Street Chapel, nevertheless remained within the congregation. They could not bring themselves to desert his ministry or to stop assembling for the preaching of the Word.

This period of ministry also had both joys and sorrows in connection with Matthew Henry's family. In 1696 he lost by death both his father-in-law, Mr Warburton, and his own father, Philip Henry. While he grieved over the death of his father-in-law after a period of considerable illness, yet his distress over his father's death was even deeper. On 23 June in the afternoon, his father's servant came to tell him of his father's illness. He hesitated at first due to it being a very wet day, but decided to hurry to Broad Oak, arriving there with Dr Tylston (his brother-in-law) about 8 pm. When his father saw him he said: 'O son, you are welcome to a dying father; I am now ready to be offered up; and the time of my departure is at hand.'[36] A little after midnight, with his wife holding his hands and his son Matthew holding the pillow at his back, he passed into the presence of his Lord. He was in his sixty-fifth year. Of his death Matthew recorded:

> He had often spoke of it as his desire, that if it were the will of God, he might not outlive his usefulness; and it pleased God to grant him his desire, and give him a short passage from the pulpit to the kingdom, from the height of his usefulness, to receive the recompence of reward. So was it ordered by him, in whose hands our times are.[37]

Matthew wrote to his father's good friend Mr Tallents, of Shrewsbury, informing him of 'the evil tidings', and saying:

---

35   Quoted in Willliams, *Memoirs*, p. 133.

36   The full account of the last words of his father are given by Matthew Henry in his biography of him, *The Life of the Rev. Philip Henry*, pp. 221-4.

37   Ibid., p. 223.

'Oh, Sir, this is a sad providence, and so sudden, that I am as one stunned. I cannot express my loss.' He told him that the funeral, the laying up of the mantle of a translated prophet, would take place the following Saturday. Mr Tallents sent a letter back to Mrs Henry, who in her reply said:

> Pray for me that I may be a widdou inded, trusting in God; that my children may, in all things, carry themselues like the children of such a father, and that wee may get the good and learne what our heavenly Fathar is teching us by this sad strok.[38]

On the Friday after his father's death Matthew should have been with his own congregation in Chester. Instead he stayed in Broad Oak, and saw the grieving congregation gather together. He remembered that his father used to say, 'Weeping must not hinder sowing', and accordingly he spent several hours in the meeting place, and preached on 2 Kings 13:20: 'Elisha died, and the bands of the Moabites invaded the land.'

The following day, Saturday, 27 June, his father was buried. His older friend, Mr Tallents of Shrewsbury, preached the sermon in the meeting house on Romans 8:23: 'And not only they, but ourselves also, which have the first-fruits of the Spirit, even we ourselves groan within ourselves, waiting for the adoption, to wit, the redemption of our body.' On the Lord's Day, Mr Owen of Oswestry preached in the morning on Elisha's farewell of Elijah (2 Kings 2:12), while Matthew Henry preached in the afternoon on Hebrews 11:4. He summarised the text by writing: *And by it he being dead yet speaketh,* ἔτι λαλεῖται is yet spoken of by us, and yet speaketh to us.'[39]

There was a very close bond between Matthew Henry and his father, and it is easy to understand the grief he expressed at his father's passing. The words he spoke to his dying father sum up the attitude he had towards him. 'Oh, Sir, pray for me that I may but tread in your steps', to which Philip Henry replied: 'Yea, follow peace and holiness, and let them say what they will.'

---

38   Ibid., p. 224.

39   Ibid., p. 229. The full text of the sermon can be found in the same volume, pp. 285-310.

This deathbed saying sums up a great deal of Philip Henry's Christian life. Though ejected from his parish he did not harbour bitterness against those who remained in the Church of England. By attending services in the Establishment he set a pattern for other Christians. His own family followed his example, and both Matthew and Sarah noted in their diaries times when they worshipped in parish churches. Sarah recalled the dying words of their father on the ninth anniversary of his death (24 June 1705):

> I cannot but remark the providence of this day nine years ago, in the surprising death of my dear and tender father, who served his generation faithfully, and naturally cared for souls. He was removed to heaven in the midst of usefulness. Oh that I may still retain the good things he taught me, and follow him who followed peace and holiness.[40]

We know that Philip was of middle stature, and almost completely bald-headed. He refused to wear a wig, saying: 'As long as I have three hairs of my own, I will never wear any body's

Matthew Henry's study.

else.' Some of his friends wanted him to have his picture drawn, but he would not allow it, maintaining that the best picture of a minister lies in the hearts of his people.[41]

At his home in Chester, Matthew Henry had a study out in the garden. This was clearly where he carried out so much

---

40 *Memoirs of Mrs Sarah Savage*, p. 186. She also notes attending the parish church at Wrenbury and being 'somewhat affected with that expression in the Common Prayer – 'Almighty God, unto whom all hearts are open, all desires known', (ibid., p. 182).

41 Ibid., pp. 233-4. A portrait claiming to be of Philip Henry exists in the National Portrait Gallery, London, but in view of Philip Henry's own position regarding a portrait, its authenticity has been doubted. However, he must have relented as portraits of him are still in the possession of descendants. In the [Dining] Hall of Christ Church, Oxford, hangs a portrait of Dr Richard Busby (headmaster of the Westminster School), along with his favourite pupil, Philip Henry.

of his literary work. Doubtless it gave him a place where he could work without distraction, for in addition to his own family he and his wife had also taken into their home four of his sister Ann's children. His sister died in 1697, while her husband died two years later. So for him, his study in the garden was a refuge in which he did an amazing amount of work. The study was still in existence in 1900, but now there is no trace of it.

Interior of the study in 1900 with chairs taken from the chapel vestry. It the lower picture is placed to the right of the upper one, three sides of the study are shown. No descriptions exist of how the study was arranged in Matthew Henry's time.

The writing of his father's biography was the first major literary work of Matthew Henry. Various friends suggested that it should be done, including Sir Henry Ashurst, who knew him both in Boreatton and in London. He pushed the idea of a biography being prepared and said of Philip Henry, 'that I loved, honoured, blessed Mr Henry; a man of so much prudence, and withal so much sincerity, of so good a temper, so much a gentleman, and yet of such strict piety and devotedness to God, that I scarce ever knew his fellow'.[42]

42   Ibid., p. 231.

Philip Henry's papers were available to his son as he set about writing his life. He did not want to write in a party spirit, for he acknowledged that his father belonged to no party except true catholic Christianity.[43] While the task must have taken immense effort in the midst of an otherwise busy life, yet the biography appeared in 1697, the year following Philip Henry's death. A second edition soon followed, correcting some mistakes in the first edition, and then after some years because it was out of print, Matthew brought out a third edition in February 1712, shortly before he left Chester to move to Hackney. He closed his preface to that edition with the deprecatory words: 'I design nothing in it but, if it may be, by the grace of God, to do good to plain people like myself.'[44]

Other bereavements came his way. In August 1697 three of his sisters were taken ill, and two of them, Ann (Mrs Hulton), and Katharine (Mrs Radford), died within three weeks of each other. He wrote in his diary: 'I find it hard to submit. Let the grace of Christ be sufficient for me. I have said it, and I do not unsay it—Lord, thy will be done.' Many children in Chester contracted measles in late 1698, and of them only one died, the Henrys' little daughter Ann. On this occasion he wrote:

> We resigned the soul of the child to Him who gave it; and, if the little ones have their angels, doubted not of their ministration in death; we have hopes, through grace, that it *is* well with the child.... We spend the day in sorrow for our affliction, our friends sympathising with us; one day committing the immortal soul to God; this day committing the dust to the dust of the earth as it was.[45]

In the following year (1699) he lost his brothers-in-law, Dr John Tylston and Mr Samuel Radford. The death of the latter meant that the four Radford children were now orphans. He and his wife were united in the decision to take these children into their own home, and they stayed with them for several years. Matthew Henry

---

43 Preface to the first edition, *The Complete Works*, vol. II, p. 603; *The Life of the Rev. Philip Henry*, p. xxxviii.

44 Ibid., p. xliii.

45 Williams, *Memoirs*, p. 72.

acknowledged that this extra work in the home did interfere to some extent with his ministerial labours, but he and his wife dealt with them so kindly that the children always spoke of the tender and affectionate way in which their uncle and aunt had cared for them.

The Henrys' own family increased further with the birth of Philip on 3 May 1700, the exact day and day of the week (Friday) on which Matthew Henry's brother John was born thirty-nine years earlier. Mother and child were both dangerously ill, and in his diary Matthew Henry recorded: 'We wept and made Supplications again and again, and we found it was not in vain.'[46]

Another four children were born to Matthew and Mary Henry. Elizabeth was born on 27 October 1701, while her sister Sarah arrived on 14 August 1703. Before they left Chester, Theodosia was born on 14 February 1708, while Mary, the last of the children, was born on 12 February 1711.

In addition to the joys of his own children, Matthew Henry had the pleasure of the love and support of his own mother until her death on 25 May 1707 at the age of 78. She was very close to her son, and was his faithful supporter, sharing his trials and being a wise and spiritual adviser to him. At the end of the year he wrote in his diary:

> I find myself growing into years, being now turned forty-five. I begin to feel my journey in my bones, and I desire to be thereby loosened from the world, and from the body. The death of my dear and honoured mother this year, has been a sore breach upon my comfort; for she was my skilful, faithful counsellor; and it is an intimation to me that now, in the order of nature, I must go next.[47]

Very little is known about Katharine Henry. Some information is available from a few of her letters that have survived, or from her husband's letters to her. For her funeral service on 4 June 1707, Matthew Henry chose his text from Proverbs 31:28: 'Her children arise up, and call her blessed.' In the course of the sermon he referred several times to his mother and commended her example.

---

46   Tong, *Life of Matthew Henry*, p. 120.

47   Williams, *Memoirs*, p. 93.

That this place has lately parted with a virtuous woman, I believe you will all own; one that was here a pious, prudent, generous, charitable housekeeper about threescore years; born here, and that here spent almost all her days, and here ended them in a good old age, with a great deal of holy security and serenity of mind. One of whom it might be said as it was of Ruth, All the children of my people do 'know that she was a virtuous woman', Ruth iii.11. You have been told of it from this place already,[48] and have been stirred up (God grant the excitement may not be in vain) to follow her and others, who are gone before us to the better country, Heb. vi.12.[49]

Later in the sermon he said:

We have reason to bless God for her that is now removed, who bid farewell to the world so very cheerfully,—said she had enough of it, and longed to be with Christ;—would not have her sickness called an affliction, but a welcome messenger to fetch her home;—and said, a little before she died, she hoped she knew, in some measure, by experience, what it is for a believer to 'have eternal life abiding in him'; having little doubt of her future happiness. For this she blessed God, and so should we.[50]

Amidst all the challenges of his pastorate and the varied experiences within his own family circle, not to mention dealing with servants in the home and on the farm, Matthew Henry turned his hand to writing biblical expositions. Even before he started what became his printed *Exposition*, Matthew Henry was in the habit of writing on Scripture. In December 1700 he sent some of these expositions to his friend, Rev. Samuel Clark. He responded, encouraging publication, but no offer from a publisher came until four years later. The most probable reason for this delay is that publishers were not willing to take the risk of accepting them, even though Matthew Henry's gifts were already widely known.

---

48   He is referring to the funeral sermon by Dr Benson.

49   *The Complete Works*, vol. II, p. 590.

50   Ibid., p. 597.

In his diary he mentioned in 1701 that he was writing notes on the Gospel of John. He confessed on the last day of that year that if he had not wasted so much of his time he would have been further on with them. On 12 November 1704 he began to write his notes on the Old Testament, completing them on 18 July 1712. Then he worked on the New Testament, reaching the end of Acts on 17 April 1714. He was not spared to write any further, and others took over the task. They based their work on notes he had made, including almost complete ones on the Epistle to the Romans. Clearly he had also spent considerable effort on the book of Revelation. He left some brief jottings on other epistles and there were also some short-hand notes of public and private expositions.[51] In all four volumes appeared during his lifetime, starting with the Pentateuch in 1706, while he had just completed the fifth volume before his death on 22 June 1714.[52]

In his notes on his ministry written in 1712, Matthew Henry had a very short statement about his *Exposition*.

> In Oct. 1706, my first volume of Expositions on the Bible came out, and in Aug. 1708, the 2nd, and in July 1710 the 3rd, Laus Deo [Praise to God]. Ps. 115.1 ['Not unto us, O LORD, not unto us, but unto thy name give glory, for thy mercy, and for thy truth's sake'].[53]

His sister Sarah Savage commenced to read through the book of Deuteronomy with her brother's annotations in November 1726. She noted that there were many excellent things in it and then recalled an incident relating to her mother. When the volume on the Pentateuch came out her mother began with Deuteronomy, giving this reason for her choice: 'I shall not live to read the whole, therefore, I take this which is the summary of the rest.'[54]

---

51 For a list of those ministers who completed the exposition of the New Testament, see Williams, ibid., p. 308.

52 For further discussion on the *Exposition*, see pp. 149-72.

53 Roberts, *Matthew Henry and His Chapel*, p. 93.

54 Mrs Savage's Diary (quoted in Roberts, *Matthew Henry and His Chapel*, p. 94).

CHAPTER 9

Final Ministry at Chester (1710-1712)

In reviewing the closing period of Matthew Henry's ministry in Chester, two aspects need special comment. First, it is clear that his health was starting to be a serious concern. As far back as 27 August 1704, while reading the Scripture during the morning service of the Lord's Day, he suddenly fainted. He recovered quickly and instead of taking this episode as a warning, he continued his busy round of engagements. The following day (Monday) he carried out a promise to preach at Nantwich, and the next day at Haslington. When he came home, however, he had a fever and was sick for over three weeks. He continued to conduct family worship, and when his sickness was over he did not wait till the Lord's Day to resume his ministry but did so for the usual midweek lecture.

From that period on, Matthew Henry's health was problematic. In his diary he often referred to health concerns, and his expectation of further afflictions and possibly death. On 1 January 1705 he wrote:

> If it be the will of God that this year should be a year of affliction to me, a year of sickness or reproach, or loss; if my family should be visited, if my liberties should be cut short, if publick troubles should arise, if any calamity should befall me, which

I am least apprehensive of now, I earnestly desire to submit to the divine disposal.... If it be the will of God that I should finish my course this year, let me be found of Christ in peace, and by the grace of God death shall be welcome to me.[1]

Later diary entries confirm that he was experiencing major health problems in the closing years at Chester.

The second matter that brought much concern to him was the number of invitations that he received to transfer to another field of labour. After his visit to London in 1698, these invitations came repeatedly. First of all, he was invited to follow Dr Bates of Hackney, and even though the request was made through one of his friends, Rev. John Shower, he declined. When Rev. Nathaniel Taylor, one of the lecturers at Salter's Hall, died, Matthew Henry was approached to accept the vacant position.[2] Even though several men wrote to encourage him, he again declined. He referred to this later in this way:

The invitation to the congregation at Salter's Hall was a surprise to me. I begged of God to keep me from being lifted up with pride by it. I sought of him a right way. Had I consulted either my own fancy, which had always a kindness to London ever since I knew it, or the worldly advantage of my family, I had closed with it; and I was sometimes tempted to think it might open a door of greater usefulness. Though I think ministers married to their ministry, yet I cannot see any scripture ground to think they are married to their people.... I bless God I am well satisfied in what I did in that matter, though it was once and again a sudden resolve. If ever it pleases God to call me from this place, I depend upon him to make my way clear. Lord lead me in a plain path.[3]

On this occasion his congregation at Chester made their feelings known that he should not accept the call. On 12 October 1702

---

1   Williams, *Memoirs*, p. 89.

2   Salter's Hall was a dissenting congregation.

3   Quoted in Williams, *Memoirs*, p. 96.

he recorded in his diary that about a dozen of the congregation had come to express the desire that he would not leave them. He went on to say: 'I assured them I had once and again given a Denial to this Invitation, that I could not tell what might happen hereafter, but that it was my present Purpose not to leave them.'[4]

The next approach was made from Manchester, and though a special delegation came to see him about the call, he again declined. He wrote: 'I cannot think of leaving Chester till Chester leaves me.' Twice in 1708 he was approached, first to accept a joint pastorship with Mr Shower at the Old Jewry, which he declined, giving the reason that he loved the people of Chester too much to leave them. Later in the same year he was approached to succeed Mr Howe at Silver Street. Numerous friends wrote to him, including William Tong and Sir Henry Ashurst, pressing him to move, but he was adamant that he was staying in Chester. That did not make people desist from trying to get him to reconsider his refusal, and this matter, with friends continuing to urge him to move, brought much uncertainty. He had anonymous letters about it, one writer even saying that he did not want him to move to London in case he did more mischief there than in Chester!

On New Year's Day, 1709, he reflected on the year that was past, and also mentioned things that were pressing on his mind and heart.

> My outward concerns, as to my health and safety, the prosperity of my affairs, provision for my family, the continuance of my life, and the lives of my relations and friends, comfort in my children and congregation, I have committed and do commit, to the conduct and disposal of God's gracious providence, which I depend upon to order every thing for good to me. Here I am, let the Lord do with me and mine as seemeth good unto him. That Providence, I trust, will so order every event as that nothing shall be an invincible temptation to me to draw me from God and duty in any instance.[5]

---

4   Quoted in Tong, *Life of Matthew Henry*, p. 342.

5   Williams, *Memoirs*, pp. 97-8.

His friend William Tong kept up the pressure on him, continuing to write pressing the claims of London. According to him everyone from Westminster to Wapping wanted Matthew to come. He reported that people wanted the Friday lecture revived and would contribute £50 a year towards doing this, and to encourage him to move from Chester they were prepared to advance fifty guineas towards his removal costs.

In his uncertainty Matthew Henry approached Dr Edward Calumy for advice. They met at Holme's Chapel in Lancashire, and this was followed up with a long letter from Calumy, trying to persuade him to reconsider his decision. In particular he attempted to get him to visit London again, saying that a little conversation was better than a hundred letters. If Matthew Henry was going to the metropolis about his book, then that would give the people who thought so highly of him the chance to say to him personally what they felt in the matter.

In the middle of 1710 the congregation of Hackney again approached him. They had obtained the ministry of Mr Billio after Matthew Henry declined the previous invitation in 1699, but on his death from smallpox the congregation again set their sights on the minister at Chester. They would not take 'no' for an answer, and some of the congregation suggested they would come to Chester and press the invitation on him. He did not want this to happen, but proposed that in the gap between the third and fourth volumes of his exposition being printed he would go down to Hackney.

He kept his word. He went to Hackney in mid-July 1710, and was back there for the first Lord's Day in August. He confessed in his diary that he had laid himself 'open to the Temptation, by encreasing my Acquaintance with the City'.[6] Various people came from London to encourage him to move to Hackney, arguing that it would be for his greater usefulness if he made the move. Hoping that he could put the Hackney congregation off, he asked them to wait till the following spring and said he

---

6   Quoted in Tong, *Life of Matthew Henry*, p. 348.

would go down for a longer trial period. That was, to Matthew Henry's surprise, acceptable to the Hackney congregation, and so in May 1711 he went down and stayed till the end of July.

While in Hackney he penned a longer paper setting out his reasons for moving from Chester to Hackney. Because it is of wider significance it is worth quoting it in full, since it reveals much of the tension in his own mind, and also contains reflections on the discouragements he had at Chester.

> Having this Morning (as often, very often before) begg'd of God to give me Wisdom, Sincerity and Humility, and to direct my Thoughts and Counsels now this important Affair must at last be determined, I think it meet, having set down the Reasons for my continuing at *Chester*, now to set down the Reasons which may induce me to accept this invitation to *Hackney*, that it may be a Satisfaction to me afterwards, to review upon what Grounds I went, and may be a Testimony for me, that I did not do it rashly.

> 1. I am abundantly satisfied that it is lawful for Ministers to Remove, and in many cases highly expedient and necessary to the edifying of the Church; and this not only for *the avoiding of Evil*, as in the case of Persecution, which can be a Reason no longer than while the Persecution lasts, or of the uncomfortable Disposition of the People, but for the attitude of a greater Good, and the putting of a Minister into a larger sphere of Usefulness; this has always been my Judgment according to the Word of God, and I have practised accordingly, in being often active to remove other Ministers which I have afterwards had Satisfaction in: And this has been the Judgment of the Congregation at Chester, between whom and their ministers there have never been those solemn mutual Engagements that have been between some other Ministers and their Congregations, nor any Bond but that of Love.

> 2. My invitation to Hackney is not only unanimous, but very pressing and importunate, and the People here in waiting so long for my Determination, and in the great

Affection and Respect they have shewed to my Ministry since I came among them, have given the most satisfying Proof of the Sincerity and Zeal of their Invitation; and upon many Weeks Trial, I do not perceive any thing in the Congregation that is discouraging, but every thing that promiseth to make a Minister's Life both comfortable and useful.

3. There seems to be something of an Intimation of Providence in many of the Calls I have had this Way before, and particularly to this Place, upon the death of Dr *Bates*, though I never either directly or indirectly sought them, but on the contrary did what I could to prevent them, and this particularly.

4. There is manifestly a much wider Door of Opportunity to do Good opened to me here in London, than is at *Chester*, in respect to the Preaching, and the great Numbers of auditors; the Prospect I have of improving these Opportunities and doing good to Souls thereby, is I confess the main Inducement to me to think of removing hither; and what I have seen while I have been here now, has very much encouraged my Expectations of that kind.

5. In drawing up and publishing Expositions, and any other of my Endeavours for the Publick Service, I foresee it will be a great convenience to me to be near the Press, and to have the Inspection of it, and also to have Books at hand that I may have occasion for in the Prosecution of my Studies, and learned Men to converse with for my own Improvement in Knowledge, and to consult with upon any Difficulty that may occur.

6. I have followed Providence in this affair, and to the Conduct of that I have (if I know my own Heart) in Sincerity referred myself, hoping and praying both myself, and my Friends for me, that God would guide me with his Eye, and lead me in a plain Path. When I was purposing to send a final Denial, Providence so ordered it, that the very Post before I had a letter subscribed by divers of the London

ministers, persuading me to accept this Call, whereupon I wrote to them that I would come to them six Months upon Trial, thinking that they would not have consented to be kept so long in Suspense, but it proved they did; and so I have been drawn Step by Step to this Resolution, and though I have industriously sought, I have not found any thing on this side to break the Treaty.

7. I have asked the Advice of Ministers, upon a fair Representation of the Case, which I drew up and many, upon Consideration that of it, have given it under their Hands that they think it adviseable to remove, and none of them have advised me to the contrary, but have told me I am myself the most proper Judge of it. Many private Christians also in London, and some that seem to be to be the most judicious and Publick-spirited, have by Letters when I was in Chester, and by Word of Mouth here, persuaded me to accept of this Call, as judging that by the Blessing of God I might be useful here to that Degree, as to balance the Inconveniency of my leaving Chester; nay, that even here I might in many respects be serviceable to the Country.

8. I have some reason to hope that my poor Endeavours in the Ministry may, by the Blessing of God, be more useful now to those to whom they are new, than to those who have been so long used to them and so constantly, with whom also I trust another Hand may do more good, as mine did by the Grace of God in the first seven Years, of my being there; And I have known many Congregations from whom Ministers have removed, and those to whom it has created the greatest Uneasiness and Discontent for the present, which yet have afterwards been so well settled beyond their own Expectations under other Ministers, that they have flourished even more than ever they had done before.

9. Tho' the People of *Chester* are a most loving people, and many of them have had, and have an exceeding Value for me and my Ministry, yet I have not been without

discouragements there, and those such as have tempted me to think that my Work in that Place has been in a great Measure done; many that have been catechiz'd with us, and many that have been long Communicants with us, have left us, and very few have been added to us.

10. Whereas I have been thought to have been useful in the Country by my Preaching, as God has enabled me in many Places about; I have now reason to think that though I should continue at Chester, I should be quite taken off from Part of my Work, having found as I came up, and once before, that riding long Journeys and Preaching brought an Illness upon me which I was never till the last Winter visited with, so that my Service would be confined wholly with the Walls of *Chester*; whereas here, by divine Assistance, I might do a great deal of Work of that kind without that Toil and Peril.

11. The congregation at Chester, tho' it cannot be expected they should consent to part with a Minister they have so long had a Satisfaction in, yet have been pleased under their Hands to leave it to my own Conscience and Affection; now as to my own Conscience, upon a long a serious Consideration of the Matter, and if I know my own Heart, (an impartial one) and after many Prayers to God for Direction, I am fully satisfied that I may *lawfully* remove, and that there is a Prospect of my being more useful if I do remove, and therefore it is *expedient* that I should; and as to my Affections, though they are very strong towards *Chester*, yet I think they ought to be over-ruled by my Judgment.[7]

Before he returned to Chester he indicated that he was accepting their invitation to be their pastor, and, God willing, he would make the move to Hackney in the spring of 1712. This decision did not end his mental distress. This is how he described the situation:

7   Ibid., pp. 349-54.

By this determination I brought on myself more grief, and care, and concern, than I could have imagined, and have many a time wished it undone again; but having opened my mouth, I could not go back. I did it with the utmost impartiality (if I know any thing of myself) beg of God to incline my heart that way which should be most for his glory; and I trust that I have a good conscience, willing to be found in the way of my duty. Wherein I have done amiss, the Lord forgive me for Jesus' sake, and make this change concerning the congregation to work for good to it.[8]

The loss of Matthew Henry as the pastor was a severe blow to the congregation, and great difficulty was found in getting a successor. From the chapel records it appears that a call was given to Mr Blackmore, of Worcester, who having preached for the congregation and given indication that he would accept a call, wrote an ambiguous letter:

... hee after holding them long in suspence sent them a letter in Octob^r following wch some tooke for a denyall & others lookt upon as dubious answer—such as his former Letters had been which occasioned a meeting of the Congregation—Octob^r 21, when it was determined by the far Major part of those present to take Mr Blackmore's answer for a denyall & to desire those entrusted by the Congregation to manage this affayr relateing to a Minister to write to Mr Aldred of Monton to request him to take on him the pastorall care & charge of the Congregation of Protestant Dissenters at Chester.[9]

The call to Mr Aldred was also declined, but finally Rev. John Gardner was installed as pastor in October 1713, and he continued to exercise his ministry until his death in November 1765. William Tong commented on Matthew Henry's concern for his former congregation, and satisfaction he felt with the settlement of Mr Gardner, with Mr Withington as his colleague from 1713 to 1720. He wrote:

---

8   Williams, *Memoirs*, p. 105.

9   Ibid., pp. 100-1.

> These Disappointments gave Mr *Henry* a great deal of Trou-
> ble, and cost him many Tears and Prayers; at length God pro-
> vided wonderfully well for them; Mr *Gardner* and Mr *Withing-*
> *ton* are Labouring among them in the Word and Doctrine with
> universal Acceptance.[10]

The next colleague, Robert Murrey, seems only to have been in
Chester a short time in 1720. He had published a book entitled
Closet Devotions in 1713 with a foreword by Matthew Henry, but
his religious convictions seem to have changed and he probably dropped out of ministry altogether. In 1737 he edited
a posthumous work by J. Platts that was very liberal in outlook.

The views of Robert Murrey and his connection with the
congregation probably presaged a change that was taking place
not only in the congregation at Chester but more widely in
English independency, as a move was under way to replace the
older Calvinism with a Socinian approach and even a Unitarian one. It is hard to be certain when the change manifested
itself unambiguously, as no written records of John Gardner's
preaching exist, and only one sermon from his successor John
Chidlaw (colleague 1751-65, sole minister 1765-98).[11]

Changes in the pulpit teaching seem to have resulted in
a secession from the congregation in 1768, though the influence
of John Wesley's ministry may also have been a contributing
factor. It is clear from his journal for Saturday, 2 April of that year,
that he preached at Little Leigh, and in the evening at Chester.
The next day, Easter Sunday, he preached again from his 'old
stand in the little Square at St Martin's Ash. The people were as
quiet as in the House'. Those who seceded formed Queen Street
Congregational Church. Whereas the trust deed of Matthew
Henry's chapel only said that it was for religious service, the
trust deed for the new congregation, drawn up in 1773, was far
more specific in its Reformed statement of the faith, and in the
demands it placed on its pastors. In the latter respect it stated:

---

10   Tong, *Life of Mathew Henry*, pp. 362-3.

11   A short extract is given in Roberts, *Matthew Henry and His Chapel*, p. 203.

... such minister to be of the Independent persuasion respecting Church government, and to hold, profess and embrace ex animo the truths comprised in the Westminster Confession of Faith & the larger and lesser Catechisms, contained therein, and also the present doctrinal articles of the Church of England in the plain, literal, and grammatical sense thereof; and no such Minister or Ministers shall be elected, nominated, and appointed as aforesaid, unless immediately before such election and appointment he shall solemnly declare in the presence of the members of the said Church or the major part of them his sincere approbation of the baptism of infants, & his renunciation of Arian, Socinian, Antinomian, or Arminian principles.[12]

Before Mr Chidlaw died he had as an assistant Rev. William Thomas, who served the congregation as its pastor from 1798 to 1809. Almost certainly the change to a Unitarian position became explicit during this ministry. No doubt exists about the views of his successor, Rev. James Lyons (1808-13), for he resigned from the Particular Baptist Church in Hull in 1807 because he was 'fully convinced there are no such doctrines in the sacred Scriptures as that of the Trinity, the equality of Jesus Christ with his Father, or of a vicarious sacrifice of his death for the sins of men'.[13] After leaving Hull he served in Scotland as a missionary for the Unitarian Fund before settling in Chester in November 1808.

Thus a congregation that had enjoyed and been blessed by Matthew Henry's biblical ministry for twenty-five years gradually moved its theological stance to become a centre of Unitarianism. Crook Street Chapel, Chester, built in 1700 to contain the growing congregation that had gathered under Mr Henry's preaching, became a congregation that boasted of its liberalism. On the occasion of the bicentenary of the congregation in 1900 one of the speakers referred to the fact that the congregation was:

---

12 Ibid., pp. 159-60.

13 Quoted from a letter he wrote to Rev. R. Wright, Wisbeach, in December, 1807. Ibid., p. 205.

always open for the free winds of heaven to blow upon them, and never submitting to any fetters, to any word of man who said, 'Thus far, and no farther'. They had undergone greater changes of belief during the past 200 years, and who knew what changes would have taken place when the tercentenary came to be celebrated?[14]

There was no tercentenary of the chapel, for by the time 2000 had come the chapel had already been demolished for thirty-six years.

---

14   Ibid., p. 229.

CHAPTER 10

Move to Hackney and Death

The various attempts that were made to induce Matthew Henry to leave Chester culminated in his acceptance of the call to the congregation in Hackney, London. His growing literary work was a factor in this move, as he was producing many other works quite apart from his commentary. He was not spared to exercise a long-term ministry there, for he died in 1714 at the age of fifty-two.

Hackney was a town on the north-east of the city of London, and it was known to be a nonconformist stronghold. Dr William Bates, after his ejection in 1662 from St Dunstan's-in-the West, had ministered in the city but later in life retired to Hackney, and there transformed some old buildings into a church that served as a dissenting meeting place for about eighty years. Bates was well known and respected by conformist and nonconformist people alike. At the Savoy conference in 1660 he rebuked some Episcopal rudeness towards Richard Baxter, and stood by Baxter when he suffered at the hands of Judge Jeffreys. The town that gave its name to Hackney coaches was noted also for the presence there of many prominent families, including that of Oliver Cromwell.[1]

---

1   For a good description of Hackney and its association with Matthew Henry, see G. Holden Price, 'Matthew Henry and the Borough of Hackney', *The Sword and Trowel*, February 1871, pp. 77-85.

The congregation to which he had come had been started in 1672 by Dr Bates, though the building in which it met had older Puritan traditions. It had been earlier used by Philip Nye and Adoniram Byfield. As compared with the congregation in Chester that Matthew Henry left, it was much smaller, having fewer than a hundred members.

His last Lord's Day at Chester was 11 May 1712, and he finished his exposition of Joshua and the Gospel of Matthew. His text for preaching in the afternoon was 1 Thessalonians 4:17-18: 'We shall be for ever with the Lord, wherefore comfort one another with these words.' How he felt is told in few but telling words: 'A very sad Day, O that by the Sadness of their Countenance and mine, our Hearts may be made better.... I see I have been unkind to the Congregation who love me too well.'[2]

On commencing his new ministry he made little change to the order of service he had used at Chester over twenty-five years. The one noticeable alteration was the commencement of the service which now became a short prayer, followed by the singing of Psalm 100. The remainder of the service followed his normal pattern. For the first Lord's Day lectures he began with Genesis 1 and Matthew 1, and he preached from Acts 16:9: 'Come over to Macedonia and help us.' He could not forget his old congregation in Chester and in his diary he wrote: 'An encouraging Auditory, O that Good may be done to precious Souls! But I am sad in Spirit, lamenting my Departure from my Friends in Chester; and yet if they be well provided for I shall be easy, whatever Discouragements I may meet with here.'[3]

Two major concerns dominated his short ministry in Hackney. The first of these was this close relationship with his former congregation in Chester and worries over who was going to minister to it. Four months after his arrival in Hackney he took part in an ordination service at St Albans. He had stayed

---

2   Tong, *Life of Matthew Henry*, p. 354.

3   Ibid., p. 355.

with Rev. and Mrs Jonathan Grew there when he was going to London in May 1698. Mr Grew had died, and Matthew Henry was there to take part in the ordination of Mr Samuel Clark as Mr Grew's successor. On the day following the ordination, he went to visit Mrs Grew, and that recalled for him his time at Chester, for his diary note was: '18. I visited Mrs Grew; looked a sorrowful look towards Chester'.[4]

As an inducement to accept the call among them, the Hackney people had suggested that he return each year to preach for several Lord's Days at Chester. He did this first in July/August 1713, setting out by coach on Monday, 20 July, and arriving in Whitchurch on Wednesday, 23 July. His welcome by old friends was a real boost for his spirits, and he preached in the afternoon at the old family home at Broad Oak. On the following Lord's Day (26 July) he preached in his old chapel from 1 Timothy 6:12: 'Lay hold on eternal life', commenting on the experience in his diary: 'It was very pleasant to preach in the old Place, where I have often met with God and been owned by him.'[5]

While he had two more Sundays in his old pulpit (2 and 9 August 1713) he preached in several other places as well, including Middlewith and Knutsford (to a meeting of ministers). He left Chester on Monday, 10 August, but not without an affectionate farewell with many friends and prayer with them. He went via Wrenbury Wood and Whitchurch, and preached at both places, before setting off on Thursday, 13 August, and reaching home on Saturday, 15 August. When he arrived home he found his Tabernacle (his congregation) at peace.

Believing God had called him to the metropolis of London, he obeyed the call but tension existed in his heart during his Hackney ministry. A multitude of ministry opportunities in London occupied him fully, but yet he seemed to yearn for his old friends in Chester. What his friend William Tong said was

---

4   Williams, *Memoirs*, p. 156.

5   Tong, *Life of Matthew Henry*, p. 364.

that 'his Spirit was much afflicted with the Thoughts of their unsettled State at Chester'.[6]

The other concern that was already there when he made the move was his own health. It is clear that he was not well when he went to Hackney. He continued his diary entries and always commented on his birthday and the first day of the new year. On 1 January 1713, just six months after he had moved south, he wrote:

> Firmly believing that my times are in God's hands, I here submit myself, and all my affairs for the ensuing year, to the wise and gracious disposal of divine providence; whether God appoint for me health or sickness, peace or trouble, comforts or crosses, life or death, his holy will be done.

On returning from his first revisit to Chester in the summer of 1713, he preached twice on the Lord's Day and administered the Lord's Supper. The next day he complained of weariness and sleepiness, and consulting Sir Richard Blackmore, diabetes was diagnosed. The doctor forbad him to go out the next Lord's Day, but a week later he was back to his normal routine. Severe attacks of kidney stones prostrated him the following month, and after passing several large stones on Sunday night and Monday, he resumed what for him was normal work – catechising in London on Tuesday, lecturing at Hackney on Wednesday, preaching on Thursday evening at Spitalfields, and on Friday preaching at a fast at Founder's Hall. On Saturday he could write: 'I bless God I have now my health well again.' At the end of that year he wrote in his diary on 13 December: 'I am very well today tho' very ill yesterday: how is this life counterchanged. Yet I am but girding on the harness. The Lord prepare me for the next fit and the last.'[7]

---

6   Ibid., p. 362.

7   Quoted by P. O. Williams, *Matthew Henry*, p. 11. The manuscript has 'fit' but the context demands 'fight'. Matthew Henry often abbreviated words and in this quotation he is referring to himself as the warrior preparing for battle.

Right from the beginning of his Hackney ministry health problems affected his work, and in his diary he noted numerous occasions when he was laid aside. But as soon as the fever, or pain from kidney stones, was over, he was back into his very busy schedule.

The move to Hackney did not bring about a lessening in his activities. He had drawn the attention of many in London from the time of his first visit as a minister in 1698. His preaching then was a talking point and one sermon was printed.[8] Six years earlier he had written in his diary: 'The Lord make me busy while working time lasts.'[9] In spite of health issues he took on more and more speaking engagements, while continuing to work on the fourth volume of his *Exposition*.

His public ministry became even busier with the move to Hackney, because he was now in much closer proximity to other Presbyterian congregations than he had been in Chester. At times he gave the Sunday morning lecture at Little St Helen's, before he returned to Hackney to take his two services. Sometimes, after his two services, he went to Wapping, or Rotherhithe, or the Charity School at Shakespear's Walk, or crossed over the water to Redriff. He was so often invited elsewhere that he was preaching practically every day of the week. The constant travel must have been very tiring, and especially as there could be danger as well. On coming to Hackney he had started catechism instruction every Saturday, but he also went into London on Tuesday to give a catechetical lecture in the chapel that once had been Dr Doolittle's place of ministry. He was returning home from his catechism exercise on Tuesday, 3 March 1713, when robbers caught him about half a mile from Hackney. They took ten or eleven shillings, and Matthew

---

8 'A Sermon showing that "The Christian Religion Is Not A Sect", and yet that it is everywhere spoken against', *The Complete Works*, vol. II, pp. 442-63.

9 His diary for 18 May 1706 is quoted in Roberts, *Matthew Henry and His Chapel*, p. 108.

Henry reflected on his experience so that it would be a blessing to him:

1. What reason have I to be thankful to God, that having travel'd so much, yet I was never Rob'd before now.

2. What abundance of Evil this Love of Money is the root of, that four Men should venture their Lives and Souls for about Half a Crown apiece.

3. See the Power of Satan working in the Children of Disobedience.

4. The Vanity of Worldly Wealth, how soon we may be stript of it, how loose we ought to sit to it.[10]

Another interest of Matthew Henry was education for children. Early in his time at Hackney he went to Gravel Lane in Southwark to preach the anniversary sermon at the school operating from the premises of Mr Marriot's congregation. His text was Proverbs 3:9, 'Honour the Lord with thy substance', and the collection was about £35. He was generous himself towards such schools, and when a large sum of money was put at his disposal, he gave £20 to a charity school.

It was a concern to him that more schools were not connected with the dissenters, that at Southwark being the only one. He prepared a paper setting out the reasons why the dissenters should establish more schools in city and country, aiming at 'Teaching of poor children to Read and Write, &c. and to cloath them and teach them the Assemblies Catechism. It is thought adviseable and not impracticable.'[11] He acknowledged with thanksgiving that many in the Church of England were engaged in this type of work. The ultimate spiritual aim was at the forefront, for he indicated how encouraging it would be for dissenting ministers 'to have such a number of young People willingly attending their Ministry, and to have an Opportunity,

10   Tong, *Life of Matthew Henry*, p. 363.

11   Ibid., pp. 358-61 gives the full text.

if it be needful, of Catechising and Instructing them publickly in the Ways of God'.[12]

He was very conscious of his incessant activity, and sometimes in his diary he comments on it. For example, on one occasion he wrote on a Lord's Day: 'I went in the Evening to open an Evening Lecture near Shadwel Church, and preached from Psalm 73:28. I hope, through Grace, I can say the Reason why I am so much in my Work is, because the Love of Christ constrains me, and I find by Experience it is good for me to draw near to God.'[13]

Matthew Henry paid his last visit to Chester in June 1714. This was again because of the promise he had made that if he accepted the call to Hackney he would come back each year to preach to his former congregation. He chose to administer the Lord's Supper to his own congregation on 30 May, before he set out on Monday 31 May for Chester. He expounded Exodus 38 in the morning and Luke 7 in the afternoon, and then preached on Revelation 5:9: 'For thou wast slain, and hast redeemed us to God by thy blood'. His friend William Tong and some others shared the coach as far as St Albans. In a letter to his wife (written on 7 June) he told her that friends at Chester told him he looked better than on his previous visit. He rejoiced in renewed fellowship with close acquaintances there. Being the first Lord's Day in the month, the Lord's Supper was observed in his old congregation, and he noted that they had a full communion, none of the congregation having gone off. He added: 'If none have left it while it was unsettled, I hope none will leave it now it is so well settled'.

Back in Chester he followed his old pattern of preaching in other congregations. On Tuesday, 8 June, he went to Wrexham and preached, going back the same night to Chester, although he did drink some bottles of Bristol Waters to prevent his diabetes returning. It is remarkable in view of his death, while

---

12 Ibid., p. 360.

13 Ibid., p. 363. Tong gives this as 25 January 1712, but Matthew Henry was not in Hackney until May 1712.

on his return journey, that on the other two Lord's Days he spent in Chester he chose texts relating to the Sabbath rest that awaits the people of God. On the first Sunday (13 June 1714) he preached on Hebrews 4:9: 'There remaineth, therefore, a rest for the people of God', while on the second (20 June 1714) he chose Hebrews 4:1 as his text: 'Let us, therefore, fear lest a promise being left us of entering into his rest, any of you should seem to come short of it.'[14]

In between the two Sundays he went first to Knutsford along with Mr Gardiner, his successor in Chester. From there he went on to Chowbent in Lancashire, returning to Chester on the Wednesday. Some of his friends thought that he did too much, especially as he complained about the hot weather, and he not only visited Wrexham, Knutsford and Chowbent but preached there as well. His thoughts, though, were with his people in Hackney. He wrote: 'Though I am here among old Friends, yet I find my new ones lye very near my Heart, among whom God has now cut out my Work.'[15]

On Saturday, 19 August, he wrote what was to be his last letter to his wife, telling her he was catching the coach on the following Wednesday and asking her to arrange some ministers to help the following week for the congregational fast. But he was never to catch the coach, as God had other things in store for him. The last earthly Sabbath he enjoyed was with his former congregation in Chester. Having recovered from his tiredness of some days previous, he arranged to preach at Nantwich en route to London. He was very sleepy on the way, but when asked about how he was he always answered, 'Well'. His ill health must have been noticeable while still at Chester as a friend, an apothecary (a pharmacist), said they would never see him again. He went by Dudden and drank a glass of mineral water, but before he came to the village of Torperley his horse stumbled in a hole and threw him. He was wet, but told

14   The notes of his sermons are given by Tong, ibid., pp. 372-85.

15   Ibid., p. 370.

his companions that he was unhurt. It is quite possible that his fall from the horse would not have happened if he had been in better health. He went on to Nantwich and preached there.

In God's providence his sister Sarah had gone to Nantwich to hear him, and she has left an account of that night.[16] When her brother reached Nantwich he hurried to the chapel, which was filled with hearers, and preached on Jeremiah 31:18: 'I have surely heard Ephraim bemoaning himself thus: Thou hast chastised me and I was chastised, as a bullock unaccustomed to the yoke; turn thou me, and I shall be turned; for thou art the Lord my God.' Her comment was: 'He did not preach with that vigour he used to have; was something short, and afterwards, exceedingly heavy and sleepy.'[17]

After the service he had dinner, and on the advice of friends he was advised to lose a little blood, even though he did not complain about his fall from the horse. He then fell asleep, but his friends thought that he was sleeping too long, and when they woke him, he was not pleased. Sir Thomas Delves and his wife had wanted Matthew Henry to spend the night at their home at Doddington, and their steward was already present to take him there. However, he was so unwell he went to bed at Rev. Joseph Mottershead's, saying to his friends, 'Pray for me, for now I cannot pray for myself'. When he was being put to bed he spoke of the spiritual comforts he had. In London he had had a conversation with his friend Mr Illidge and gave him this saying or motto: 'That a holy, heavenly life, spent in the service of God and communion with him, is the most pleasant and comfortable life any one can live in this world.'[18] He had

---

16 It is printed as an appendix in J. B. Williams, *Memoirs of the Life and Character of Mrs Sarah Savage*, pp. 242-8.

17 Ibid., p. 243.

18 This is the form in which the motto is given by his sister Sarah in her diary, p. 247. A slightly different one is given by Tong, *Life of Matthew Henry*, p. 387. Several writers indicate that this was his deathbed saying, but the evidence is clear that he had spoken it earlier in London.

a restless night, and about 5 o'clock in the morning he took a stroke, and about three hours later passed away.

The following day his sister Sarah came to view his body and wrote about her experience in these terms:

> I went to the place to take leave of the dear earthen vessel, in which was lodged such a treasure, and shall always remember there was nothing of death to be seen in his face, but rather something of a smile. How is the gold become dim, and the fine gold changed! .... I have reason to think he loved me the best of all his sisters, and it is with satisfaction I think of the love I had for him, and the great unity that was amongst us then, so that I do not remember one angry or unkind word betwixt us. O how happy a thing it is thus to dwell, and not to have the sting of any unkindness in the reflection. Though I well remember that I have thought my dear mother had most tenderness and love for my brother, yet I was so far from envying for his sake, that I complied with her, and loved him with a pure heart fervently.[19]

On that same day the minister of the local Baptist congregation noted the loss sustained by the passing of such a person, while on Thursday of that week Mr Reynolds preached in the chapel at Nantwich from the words, 'Well done, good and faithful servant', showing 'that our Lord Jesus will certainly come again, and reward all his true and faithful servants, and those whom he blesseth, are blessed indeed'.[20] On Friday, 25 June, the body was taken from Nantwich to Chester, being met on arrival there by eight of the Anglican clergy, ten coaches and many horses, many dissenting ministers and other mourners. The body was laid to rest in Trinity Church beside his first wife. Sarah reflected in her diary on the circumstances of her brother's death: 'As to the manner of his death (being on a journey and amongst strangers) I doubt not God had wise and holy ends in so ordering it. Sad,

---

19 *Memoirs of the Life and Character of Mrs Sarah Savage*, pp. 243-4.

20 Ibid., p. 245.

sad, sad tidings to his poor family.'[21]

The fact that Matthew Henry's body was interred in an Anglican church is testimony to the respect with which he was held, even by churchmen who differed sharply from him. Trinity Church is no longer used for religious worship, having become the Guildhall. The graves of Matthew Henry and his wife are covered by the reconstruction of the sanctuary to form a conference hall. Within the altar rails a small brass plaque was placed with an inscription in Latin, which translated as follows:

Memorial to Matthew Henry almost opposite Chester Castle. It was erected in 1860, and contains his name, dates, and gives to him the title V. D. M (Latin, *verbi dei minister*), minister of God's Word.

> Near this place are deposited the mortal remains of Katherine Henry, only daughter of Samuel Hardware, Esq, and the tenderly beloved wife of Matthew Henry, Minister of the most holy gospel, who, at the birth of her first child (a daughter, who survived); falling a victim to the small-pox, removed to her heavenly home, February, the 14th, 1688-89, aged twenty-five years.
>
> This monument was raised, in the deepest affliction, by her bereaved husband.

---

21   Ibid., p. 246.

The above-mentioned Matthew Henry having
assiduously fulfilled the duties of a
Christian and a Minister, his body, exhausted
by the labour he devoted to the study and
interpretation of the most holy Scriptures,
was committed to this tomb, June 22nd, in the
year 1714, and in the fifty-second year of
his age.[22]

One son, and five daughters, by Mary,
daughter of Robert Warburton Esq., now a
mourning widow, survive him.

On the following Lord's Day at Nantwich Mr Mottershead preached on the text 'My father, my father, the chariots of Israel, and the horsemen, thereof' (2 Kings 2:12), while the following Lord's Day at Chester Mr Gardner, Matthew Henry's successor, used the same text, while his assistant, Mr Worthington, spoke on the words of our Saviour when on the way to the cross: 'Weep not for me, but for yourselves, and your children' (Luke 23:28).

No record exists of how the news of his death reached his wife and family in Hackney. William Tong said that there was 'universal concern and sorrow', so much so that there was hardly a dissenting congregation in London that failed to take notice:

of the great Breach that was made upon the Church of God; every sermon was a Funeral Sermon for Mr Henry, he was universally Lamented, and those that are no Friends to the Nonconformists, readily acknowledged, that we had lost one that was an Honour and Support to our weak and despised interest.[23]

---

22 A discrepancy occurs regarding the date of his burial. He died on Tuesday, 22 June 1714, and he was buried in Chester on Friday, 25 June 1714. The memorial tablet is now inaccessible. It may contain a wrong date, or else J. B. Williams made the mistake in transcribing it.

23 Tong, ibid., p. 391.

William Tong does make just a passing reference to the family, saying that Matthew Henry's death was a deep wound, and at the time of the publication of his book (two years afterwards) 'it is fresh and bleeding still'.[24] He has another reference to Mary Henry when writing about the happiness of her marriage to Matthew. He comments on the fact that he was 'a prudent, faithful, kind Husband', and then adds:

> I need not enlarge, the Sorrows, I had almost said, the immoderate Sorrows of her that survives him, (besides many other Witnesses) too plainly shew the Sense she has how great a blessing she had in him, and how happy they were in each other; his Letters, his Diary, all his Papers are full of the most convincing tokens of his most affectionate regard to her on all occasions.[25]

Mary Henry was left a widow with seven surviving children. She survived her husband for seventeen years, dying in August 1731. Her sister-in-law, Sarah Savage, noted in her diary on 12 August: 'Thursday morning dear sister Henry begun her everlasting rest. To her a merciful release, having been seven months confined. She was in her sixty-third year. Mr Gardner's text was Ps. lxiii.3. "Thy loving kindness is better than life."'[26] The fact that Rev. John Gardner preached at the funeral indicates a return of Mary Henry to Chester after Matthew Henry's death. His son, Philip Warburton,[27] was elected to represent Chester in Parliament in 1747, again pointing to residence in Chester prior to that.

---

24   Ibid.

25   Ibid., p. 143.

26   This excerpt is quoted in Williams, *Memoirs*, p. 299.

27   For his change of name, see p. 41.

CHAPTER 11

Matthew Henry the Preacher

From an early age Matthew Henry's heart was turned towards the work of the ministry. He was touched spiritually at a very young age by his father's preaching. Philip Henry encouraged his children to prepare for the Lord's Day by spending an hour together every Saturday afternoon. At these times Matthew Henry presided, being the eldest and a boy. If he thought his sisters had cut short their prayers he would gently reprove them!

After his period of legal study in London (April 1685 to June 1686) he returned to his parents' home at Broad Oak in June 1686 and immediately commenced preaching. The way his preaching was received and the effect it had on a notoriously godless couple seem to have confirmed his sense of calling to the ministry.

Matthew Henry's sermons on the Covenant of Grace, showing the minute size of his sermon notes.

On a visit to Chester he was invited to preach and did so on several consecutive evenings. The dissenters who heard him issued an invitation to him to become their pastor. After consulting his father he accepted the invitation, but sought a little time as he wished to return to London for some months. It was there that he was ordained privately by a gathering of Presbyterian ministers on 9 May 1687. He commenced his ministry at Chester on Thursday 2 June 1687 by giving the normal Thursday lecture.

From that time onwards Matthew Henry was busy with preaching and lecturing in his own congregation and at many other places near Chester. Within his own congregation at nine o'clock on Sunday morning, in addition to psalm singing and prayer, he both lectured on a portion of the Old Testament (that is, gave an exposition) and also preached a sermon. The same sort of pattern was followed in the afternoon, though he lectured on the New Testament at that service. During the course of his ministry at Chester he went through the whole of the Bible with his congregation more than twice. On Thursday evening he also lectured, and his expositions on Scripture questions took twenty years. While the actual attendances at these various services are unknown, the fact that his congregation grew until it had over three hundred and fifty communicants testifies to the appreciation of his ministry. Also, the increase in seating capacity by the building of a gallery in the chapel was because of growing attendances.

His diary reveals that he was also extremely active in preaching in villages around Chester. In Moldsworth, Grange, Bromborough, Elton and Saighton he preached every month, but even more frequently in Beeston, Wrexham, Stockbridge and Darnal. Each year he paid a visit to Nantwich, Newcastle and Stone, and towards the end of his ministry in Chester he went every year on a preaching tour in Lancashire. Shrewsbury, Market Drayton and Stafford were also on his list of preaching appointments. On several occasions he went to London, preaching at various places on the way, and in the metropolis he preached practically every day of his visit.

From the time he first preached in London in 1698 he was a popular preacher in the metropolis. When he moved to Hackney in 1712 his frequency of preaching was in no way reduced.

He had a smaller congregation than at Chester (about 100 communicants), but requests for him to preach or lecture were numerous. In spite of his ill health (diabetes and kidney stones were among his ailments) he constantly accepted opportunities to minister in other chapels or meeting places. Doubtless the fact that the author of *The Exposition of the Old and New Testaments* was ministering in such close proximity to the city of London meant that many invitations would be directed to him. More than once he gave the morning lecture at Little St Helens, and then went back out to Hackney and delivered his usual two lectures and two sermons. On returning to his home in the evening, he conducted his normal family worship. Many weeks he was lecturing or preaching every day, either in his own congregation or in other dissenting chapels.

In planning his preaching at Chester, Matthew Henry was very systematic.[1] His first series of sermons was on the misery of being in a sinful state. He followed on with sermons dealing with conversion, and this took him two years. Then came a series of sermons in which he laid down the biblical pattern of Christian conduct expressed in twenty statements that he expounded with an appropriate text for each head. After that he wanted to bring comfort to God's people and therefore entered on his long series on the covenant of grace, in which he dealt in order with 'God in the Covenant', 'Christ in the Covenant', 'The Holy Spirit in the Covenant', and 'Peace in the Covenant'. At the end of this series, as with all his other ones, he preached a sermon or two summarising the content of the preceding sermons and recapitulating the main points.

Not a great deal can be gleaned about his pulpit style as he preached. Early on, his speech was rapid, and indications exist that he was vigorous in his delivery. Once he said in a sermon: 'You think we are *too* earnest with you to leave your sins and accept of Christ; but when you come to die, you will see the

---

1   For a list of his sermons, see Williams, *Memoirs*, note F, pp. 273-93.

meaning of it. We see death at your backs.'[2] A letter from his father to him suggests that he was extremely active in the pulpit as he pressed home the application of his sermons. He had been laid aside by extreme exertion in the middle of 1688 (only one year after his settlement in Chester). His father gave him this advice:

> ... And sure you should bee careful of yourself, for Prayers ought to be seconded with endeavours; I doe not mean that you should spare yours[elf] in the sense in which the Satan spoke to Peter, for I see our Opportunities passing away, & I cannot say, whatever others think, that you doe too much and should abate; but one thing, which I gave you a hint of, when with you, I again mind you of, & that is, in the loose you take, in your earnestness, keep the reines upon it, & let it neither run too far, nor last too long; for I have mys[elf], by experience found some prejudice by it, especially in my sight.[3]

His friend William Tong said that he had 'a mighty Warmth of Spirit both in praying and in preaching, which would often, especially in his younger years, transport him into Tears, and raise the auditory to the same pitch of affection'.[4] In his diary for 10 September 1699, Matthew Henry noted that he preached that day on Psalm 73:26, 'Whom have I in heaven but thee? And there is none on earth that I desire besides thee'. He added:

> I had some enlargement of Affections and I find some preju-
> dice to my bodily Strength by my Over-earnestness, but I can-
> not help it, for I believe the Things that I speak to be true and
> great, and I would be in my Work as one that is in earnest.[5]

The fact that his preaching was so popular, not only in Chester and the surrounding areas but in London also, suggests that his

---

2   Ibid., p. 114.

3   Lee, *Diaries and Letters of Philip Henry*, p. 361.

4   Tong, *Life of Matthew Henry*, p. 161.

5   Ibid., p. 162.

content and style attracted many. These included not just the common people but titled ones also. In his diary on 22 January 1709 he noted that Lord James Russell's wife requested him to give her a copy of his sermon notes on Job 18:4. On another occasion he was preaching in London and the Countess of Oxford was at his morning lecture.

Matthew Henry's chapel, Chester, with a view of the pulpit from the vestry door, and also showing the tablet in his memory.

In many respects Matthew Henry's sermons were typical of the Puritan period.[6] The Puritans believed that preaching is vital in that it is the unfolding of God's Word so that its teaching is plain to the minds of hearers. It is the principal way God has ordained of bringing His life-giving Word home to humans. Zwingli began the practice of regular and consecutive exposition of Scripture, but it was the Cambridge Puritans who developed it most fully. Matthew Henry followed in their shoes as he opened up the Scriptures to his hearers. Like the other Puritans he was not averse at all to doctrinal preaching, for he held to the evangelical and reformed position of the Protestant

---

6   For discussion of Puritan preaching, see Peter Lewis, 'The Puritan in the Pulpit' in his book *The Genius of Puritanism* op. cit., pp. 19-52; J. I. Packer, 'Puritan Preaching' in *A Quest for Godliness*, pp. 277-89.

Reformation and believed wholeheartedly that the theology of the Scriptures is to be preached to sinners and saints.

Three further points should be made about his sermons. First, he was methodical, not only in planning and preparing his sermons, but also in his presentation of the biblical content. Peter Ramus, a Huguenot academic, had taught that analysis is the key to understanding, and the Puritans took up this point and utilised it with their orderly presentation of material. This was intended to make the matter plain to hearers and to help them to remember it better. Matthew Henry has been criticised for overuse of alliteration, but alliterated headings certainly made memorisation of the main point of sermons very much easier.

Secondly, Matthew Henry followed the other Puritans in always seeking to press home the teaching of Scripture to his hearers. His sermons never ended without some practical application. The teaching of Holy Scripture was not just of theoretical concern but something that should move hearers to action. Even the children were not left out of his direct appeals. In a sermon on 'Christ's Favour to Little Children' (Mark 10:16) he spoke directly to the children before he addressed the parents on their duties. To the children he said:

> You hear, dear little ones, what Christ has done for you, what favour he has showed to those of your age: and will you not put in for an interest in his favour, and the provision he has made for the entertainment of children? Has he thus loved you, and will you not love him? Has he such kind thoughts toward you, and will not you have dutiful thoughts towards him? Does he not invite you to him, and will not you accept of his invitation?[7]

Thirdly, there is one respect in which Matthew Henry differs from his Puritan predecessors. Whereas they often chose to deal with a particular topic and preached week after week from the same text, he chose to preach from different texts even

---

7 *Family Religion*, pp. 116-17.

if he was dealing with the same subject. This gave greater variation to his preaching, and brought out even more broadly the biblical teaching on the matter at hand. It is not surprising that his preaching appealed to so many in his day and, being delivered with simplicity and wonderful turns of phrase, his sermons struck home to the consciences of hearers.

Anyone already familiar with Matthew Henry's commentary or his other works will find here the same style in his sermons. He knew his Bible exceptionally well, referring constantly to other biblical passages. He studied the Scriptures intently, and organised his material methodically. Constantly he illustrated, not by lengthy stories, but by phrases and references that crystallised his points. Above all, he pressed home the truth to his listeners (and readers). He also knew and utilised the great Christian writings from the early church down to his day.

In his *Complete Works* nearly all the sermons included are those delivered at special occasions, such as ordinations of ministers or funeral orations. Among the latter is the sermon he preached on the death of his mother. He was certainly very popular as a preacher, and many requests were made to him to preach at significant events. In view of the number of marriages at which he was present, it is surprising that none from these occasions are included in *The Complete Works*. The only one to survive is printed at the end of the volume of his sister Sarah's *Diary*.[8] What that reveals is that he adopted his usual practice and simply chose a text appropriate to the occasion and preached on it. The date of this sermon is given as 6 November 1684, which, if correct, means that it was delivered when he was only 22 years old and still single. Another oddity is that the preacher is described as *Rev.* Matthew Henry, though he was not ordained until 1687. If the date is correct, then this was a sermon preached at a marriage some months before he went to London for the second time in

---

8 'A Sermon, Preached at a Wedding, Nov. 6, 1684, by the Rev. Matthew Henry', Appendix II, Williams, *Memoirs of the Life & Character of Mrs Sarah Savage*, pp. 225-42.

April 1685. Features of the sermon suggest that it was from the early date, as it is not as full as many of his later sermons. The designation 'Rev.' may simply be because the sermon was printed at a date after his ordination.

If this sermon is typical of his wedding sermons, he was very direct in his teaching about commitment to Christ. He believed that two characteristics in particular belong to the Christian family, for he told the couple, and whoever else was present, that every Christian home needs a throne and an altar.[9] What he meant, of course, was that first of all the Lord Jesus has to be head of the home. 'God will have the uppermost place in the heart, and in the house too, or else he will have none; for God will come no where to be an underling. Now what do you say to this? Are you willing to have him upon these terms? Will you promise that, by the grace of God, sin shall not rule you, the world shall not rule you?' Secondly, by having an altar he meant that the family must have regular worship. To the couple, Matthew Henry said: 'If you would have God to dwell with you, you must set up and keep up, the daily worship of God in your families.... Pray with your families. Read the Scriptures to them, and sing Psalms.'

The only continuous series of sermons extant is the one on the covenant of grace.[10] In this we have a consecutive series of sermons on a particular theme, accompanied by a closing sermon that summarises the content of the whole series.

There are remarks on biblical passages that many readers will recognise from his commentary, for, as already indicated, clearly his sermon preparation lay behind much of his other writing. Many notable expressions like these occur:

---

9   Ibid., pp. 239-40. Matthew Henry also preached a sermon on 1 Cor. 16:19, 'With the church that is in their house'. This sermon, entitled 'A Church in the House: A Sermon concerning Family Religion', appears in *The Complete Works*, pp. 248-267. It is also to be found in Matthew Henry, *Family Religion*, pp. 27-64.

10   Allan M. Harman, ed., *The Unpublished Sermons of Matthew Henry on the Covenant of Grace*.

God's beloved ones are the world's hated ones and we are not to marvel at it.

When we come for the pardon of our sins we must come with a Christ in the arms of our faith and love.

In the want of the faith of assurance live by the faith of adherence.

Are you in doubt about your spiritual state? Put the matter out of doubt by a present consent—if I never did, I do it now.[11]

Every transgression in the covenant doth not put us out of covenant. Especially understand that our salvation is not in our own keeping but in the hands of the mediator.

We have *all* received the Gospel. Salvation is a *common* salvation (Jude 3). All have need to receive, even the most worthy. All are welcome to receive, even the most unworthy, if they come and seek it in the right way.

Assure yourselves none shall come to heaven hereafter but those that are fitted for it by grace here. 'Tis only the pure in heart that shall see God (Matt. 5:8; Heb. 12:14).

Believe that you have a holy God above you, a precious soul within you, and an awful eternity before you, either of weal or woe.

Our rule is to do as we would be done by, not as we are done unto.

God will break those hearts that will never bend.

Grow upwards in heavenly mindedness, downward in humility. Be pressing forward. The way to grow in grace is to use what we have. The Word is the means of our growth. Make daily use of it (2 Tim. 3.17).

---

11   This seems to have been a favourite saying of his, as he used it when he was describing his own spiritual situation when he was only ten years old. See Williams, *Memoirs*, p. 5.

There are sufficient sermons of Matthew Henry available to enable judgments to be made concerning them. They are testimony to a faithful gospel preacher, who, with a mind and heart set on the things of God, sought to unfold the riches of Scripture. They are not just relics of the past, but will speak God's Word to the present-day reader just as his *Exposition* continues to do.

CHAPTER 12

Matthew Henry the Commentator

Matthew Henry occupies a unique place in church history, because of the widespread use of his commentary, and to a lesser extent of some of his other writings. His name is known, even if his writings are not read! However, there is evidence that even three hundred years after his commentary was first published Christians are still using it, in spite of all the others available. This is what J. I. Packer has written:

> For the record (though I do not suppose I am typical in this), modern expositions do not help me half as much as does Matthew Henry, the Puritan, and modern printed sermons do not suggest to me half as much as do those of C. H. Spurgeon and the sermonic writings of J. C. Ryle.[1]

His commentary on the Bible has a clarity about it that makes it so readable, and the spiritual tone of it is so warm that it has continued to speak to successive generations.

The *Exposition* was the outcome of his years of regular lecturing to his congregations, and thus it was already tested in a setting with a wide cross-section of hearers. In addition, it

---

1   J. I. Packer, *Honouring the Written Word of God: Collected Shorter Writings of J. I. Packer*, vol. 3, p. 335.

was not just annotations on the text of Scripture but was a continuous commentary on every verse. This meant that Matthew Henry's work was, for his day, in a category of its own. As one of his successors in evangelical ministry in Chester wrote, Matthew Henry 'did what was never done before; he made the labours of successors comparatively light, as well as gave to the people at large a treasure which they will be slow to part with'.[2]

1. The Commentator

Matthew Henry's work as a commentator cannot be understood in isolation, for his work is the fruit of developments that go back to the Renaissance and Reformation periods. The humanists who lived and worked prior to the Reformation pioneered an approach to ancient documents that had direct impact on the work of biblical scholars and theologians, and a new exegetical approach superseded the barrenness of the medieval exegesis of Scripture.

Nicholas of Lyra (c. 1270-1349), a French Francisan, was one of the few medieval scholars who protested against the forced scheme of exegetical method practised in his day. In the preface to his commentaries, he complained that 'the literal sense is nearly suffocated among so many mystical expositions'.[3] In this judgment he was unusual, for a century later Paul of Burgos, in an additional preface to the same work, sharply repudiated Lyra's too great concern with the literal sense. The resulting methods of biblical interpretation by the end of the fifteenth century were described by Geiler of Kaiserberg as making the Bible a nose of wax.[4] The old idea of the literal sense being inferior lingered on. Teachers spoke as though 'the spiritual sense' was 'higher' or 'nobler' than the literal. In the

---

2   C. Chapman, *Matthew Henry, His Life and Times: A Memorial and a Tribute* (London: Arthur Hall, Virtue & Co., 1859), p. 134.

3   Quoted by Basil Hall, *Cambridge History of the Bible* (Cambridge: CUP, 1976), vol. 3, p. 79.

4   ibid.

medieval schools at first sentences such as Peter Lombard's were used. Then fuller commentaries on the biblical books appeared, especially on the Psalter and the Pauline epistles. The Latin text was used almost exclusively except when there was a revival of biblical learning about the early fourteenth century with the Oxford Dominican, Nicholas Trevet, and Nicholas of Lyra being the outstanding figures.[5]

While there is no direct connection between the humanists and the Reformers, there is definitely an indirect link. The Renaissance movement paved the way by insisting on the need to get back to the sources (*ad fontes*), and helped by providing the tools that were needed for biblical research (texts, grammars, lexicons). However, there were many in the Renaissance movement who were secular in their orientation, and their philosophical approach (including Neo-Platonism) was antithetical to what the Reformers were aiming for. In the case of Luther and Calvin their humanist training was certainly applied very productively to their work, and this helps to explain the enduring nature of their biblical exegesis. While it is not true to say that there would never have been a reformation without the Renaissance, it is true that the Reformation took the precise form it did because its approach to the biblical text was one which was developed from principles set out by the humanist scholars in their return to the sources.

Care must be taken, however, lest we overemphasise how far the pre-Reformation scholars came towards an exegetical method similar to that used by Luther and Calvin. A good illustration is the case of Wycliffe. While he was a product of his time, yet he did insist that philosophy had to be subordinate to biblical teaching. In saying this he was taking a position later followed by the Reformers as they attacked the secularism of the Renaissance humanism. But in many ways Wycliffe was still working within the framework of the medieval system of

---

5   See Beryl Smalley, *Study of the Bible in the Middle Ages* (Oxford: Blackwells, 1952), pp. 216-19.

thought. In commenting on the Old Testament he was heavily dependent on the medieval scholars. Beryl Smalley has described his recipe for writing as follows: 'use Auriol's *Compendium* as a mould, pour in [Nicolas of] Lyre, flavour with Augustine, and sprinkle with Grosseteste'.[6] Gerald Bray's judgment on him is good:

> However, we should not forget that Wycliffe was still a child of the Middle Ages, and we must not be surprised to discover that his practice of biblical exegesis often fell short of his principles. He accepted figurative meanings in Scripture, and used allegory on occasion, in ways which would not be accepted a century or more later. Wycliffe was a pioneer of something new, but his ideas had to wait for nearly 150 years before they were able to bear lasting fruit.[7]

Matthew Henry's work has also to be set in its context as part of the Puritan movement of biblical exposition and proclamation. There is a direct connection between the method of biblical exposition used by the Puritans and that of the Reformers. They carried on the approach to the Bible established by Luther and Calvin and their fellow reformers, and so approached Scripture seeking to interpret it literally and grammatically. Though Matthew Henry did not personally sit at the feet of the great Puritans, yet his father Philip had, and so he was influenced by their approach. To understand their approach to the task of expounding Scripture they asked in essence several questions of the text:[8]

1. What do these words actually mean?

2. What light do other Scriptures throw on this text? Where and how does it fit into the total biblical revelation?

---

6   Ibid., p. 256. Robert Grosseteste (c. 1175-1253) was an English biblical scholar who lectured in Oxford and was latterly Bishop of Lincoln.

7   Gerald Bray, *Biblical Interpretation: Past and Present* (Downers Grove: IVP, 1996), p. 155.

8   I take these from J. I. Packer's discussion on 'The Puritans as Interpreters of Scripture', *A Quest for Godliness*, p. 105.

3. What truths does it teach about God, and about man in relation to God?

4. How are these truths related to the saving work of Christ, and what light does the gospel of Christ throw upon them?

5. What experiences do these truths delineate, or explain, or seek to create or cure? For what practical purpose do they stand in Scripture?

6. How do they apply to myself and others in our own actual situation? To what present and human condition do they speak, and what are they telling us to believe and do?

As already mentioned, the views of Peter Ramus, influential on 16th European philosophers, also affected the Puritans. This resulted in them setting out their material logically, so that they had headings, sub-headings and sub-sub-headings! What was behind this method was the understanding that there is an intellectual element in presenting the gospel. Unless preaching touches the mind first, then the emotional and volitional response to the message will be distorted. Matthew Henry's systematic and logical approach is evident both in his commentary and in his sermons. He follows the Puritans' stress on the intellectual character of ministry, both spoken and written. Preaching in the Reformed tradition 'was the product of arduous mental exercise, and it was designed to provoke an exercise of mind in those to whom it was addressed. These men were concerned with truth. Their view of the gospel was that it is the truth "as it is in Jesus", and it is therefore as truth that it must be declared. Truth demands understanding in the preacher, and is addressed to the understanding of the hearer'.[9]

Clearly Matthew Henry had a remarkable knowledge of the Bible, first of all in the form of the *Authorised Version* of 1611. He knew it intimately and also its marginal readings. The AV

---

9   J. A. Caiger, 'Preaching—Puritan and Reformed', in *Press Towards the Mark: Papers read at the Puritan and Reformed Studies Conference, 19th and 20th December, 1961*, p. 54.

translators say in their preface: 'If you ask what they had before them, truly it was the Hebrew text of the Old Testament, the Greek of the New .... If truth be tried by these tongues, then whence should a translation be made, but out of them.' Matthew Henry from an early age was a scholar of Hebrew and Greek, and without parading his learning he draws upon it in his exegesis.

Just as it is important to note the developments in exegetical work that preceded and influenced Henry, so the fact that the Puritan influence continued and in a sense came to a climax in the ministry of Charles Simeon (1759-1836) in Cambridge must also be noted.[10] Whereas the Puritans spoke of 'opening up the text', Simeon spoke of bringing 'out of the Scriptures what is there'. There are three things that are indispensable in a sermon according to Simeon. First, there must be *unity* in design; secondly, there must be *perspicuity* in the arrangement; and thirdly, there must be *simplicity* in diction.[11]

2. His Commentary on Holy Scripture

The Reformation brought a tremendous change in regard to biblical exposition. The medieval practice of allegorising the text was set aside in favour of grammatico-historical exegesis. This meant that an expositor approached a biblical passage and worked through it in the original language. Questions of grammar and philology were discussed and the passage was placed in its historical context. Only then was the teaching of the passage set out and also utilised in later theological formulations. John Calvin brought to the task his skills as a Renaissance scholar and his commentaries on the biblical text became the model for later commentaries. By Matthew Henry's time there were not only the Reformation commentaries as exemplars but those from the post-Reformation and Puritan periods.

---

10   See the discussion on Simeon by J. I. Packer, 'Expository Preaching: Charles Simeon and Ourselves,' in *Honouring the Written Word of God: Collected Shorter Writings of J. I. Packer*, vol. 3, pp. 269-76.

11   See his *Horae Homilecticae*, vol. I, p. vi (Preface).

The commentary of Matthew Henry fits easily into the category of Puritan exposition of Scripture. Many of the great Puritans had already died before he was born, but through his father he had contact with their ideas and works. His commentary is thus representative of what was at the essence of Puritan biblical study and exposition. Underlying all the Puritan efforts were the basic presuppositions of the divine nature of the Bible and the fact that biblical doctrine was the teaching regarding God and what duty He required of man. The Puritans clearly taught that man unaided by the Holy Spirit could not understand biblical teaching, for it was spiritually discerned.[12]

In commencing his great task Matthew Henry thought it necessary to spell out the six great principles that were his presuppositions. They were:

1. That religion is the one thing needful.

2. That divine revelation is necessary to true religion.

3. That divine revelation is not now to be found nor expected anywhere but in the Scriptures of the Old and New Testament.

4. That the Scriptures of the Old and New Testaments were purposely designed for our learning.

5. That the holy scriptures were not only designed for our learning, but are the settled standing rule for our faith and practice.

6. That therefore it is the duty of all Christians diligently to search the Scriptures, and it is the office of ministers to guide and assist them therein.[13]

---

12   For an excellent discussion of the Puritan exposition of Scripture see J. I. Packer, 'The Puritans as Interpreters of Scripture,' in *A Quest for Godliness*, pp. 97-105. It is also available in a slightly different form in *Puritan Papers vol. 1 1956-1959*, ed. D. Martyn Lloyd-Jones (Phillipsburg: P & R Publishing, 2000), pp. 191-201.

13   *Matthew Henry's Commentary*, vol. 1, pp. xcix-ci.

Two aspects are important in considering the background to the expository work of Matthew Henry. The first is the influence of his father, Philip Henry. Apart from help from a young tutor who was living with the Henry family, and a few weeks at Dr Doolittle's academy in Islington, all of Matthew's biblical and linguistic training was done by his father. His father had the advantage of great schooling at the Westminster School, London, under Dr Richard Busby. A portrait of Dr Busby hangs in the [Dining] Hall of Christ College, Oxford, in which he is shown with his favourite pupil, Philip Henry. At Oxford, Philip had further classical and biblical training, and then used that training in his ministry, for the short time at Worthenbury, and then as a dissenter from 1662 till his death in 1696.

This means that Matthew Henry was exposed to his father's education up till the time he went to London to study law in 1685. In addition he listened to his father expounding the Scriptures in the family all that time, as well as hearing him lecture and/ or preach on many Sundays. It would be most surprising if he did not pick up many of his father's ideas and expressions. This is confirmed by examination of the *Exposition* as compared with passages in his father's work. While the extant work from Philip Henry is much more restricted than that of his son, yet it is sufficient to help in this regard. Matthew Henry's comment on Genesis 2:21 is often quoted. This is what he wrote:

> 4.   That the woman *was made out of the side of Adam*, not made out of his head to rule over him, nor out of his feet to be trampled upon by him, but out of his side to be equal with him, under his arm to be protected, and near his heart to be beloved.[14]

It is clear that he borrowed the ideas here from his father. A manuscript survived of his father's exposition in the handwriting of Matthew at the age of twenty, and it was published in 1829. This is what Philip Henry wrote on this verse:

---

14   ibid., p. 16.

Adam lost a rib, but he got a better thing out of it, even a help meet for him. Thus God uses [is accustomed] to deal with his children: they lose sometimes some of their creature-comforts; but then perhaps they get more of the Creator's comforts, and that's a blessed exchange. This bone was taken out of Adam's side, fitly noting the woman's place; not out of his head, to be above him; not out of his feet, to be trampled on by him; nor from before him, as his better; nor from behind him, as his servant;—but out of his side, to be equal with him; near his heart, for he owes her love; under his arm, for he owes her protection. Surely they forget from whence the woman was taken, that carry themselves haughtily and abusively towards their wives.[15]

This should not be regarded as plagiarism on Matthew Henry's part. Being so often exposed to his father's thoughts, it was only natural that they would be reflected in his work. He does not take over his father's words exactly, but adapts the idea to fit in with his exposition.

The second major factor behind his work as a commentator was his own experience as a pastor and father. He followed his father's custom in regard to family worship, and consequently he expounded the Scripture twice a day in his family circle. He also modelled his ministry on his father, and so lectured on Old and New Testament chapters every Lord's Day to his congregation. In his pastorate at Chester (1687-1712) he covered the entire Bible more than twice. By the time he formally started on his *Exposition* in 1704, he had already been a pastor for seventeen years, and in addition to his lectures, had preached extensively over Scripture.

These two factors (his father's training and his own ministry) worked together to produce a mind and heart well prepared for commenting on the Bible. They also explain the width of literature that he was able to draw upon and use fruitfully in his writing. First of all, he was very familiar with Latin and

---

15   Philip Henry, *An Exposition with Practical Observations, upon the First Eleven Chapters of the Book of Genesis*, p. 56.

Greek classical writers, such as Plutarch, Cicero, Seneca and Epictetus, and also the Jewish historian Josephus. From the church fathers he quotes writers such as Tertullian, Chrysostom and Augustine. He knew the Reformers and the post-Reformation writers well, quoting Bishop Patrick, Daniel Whitby, Dr Lightfoot, Joseph Caryl, George Fox and Joseph Hall. The comments of Hall (1574-1656), Bishop of Norwich, on the historical passages of the Old and New Testaments seem to have been very influential on him.[16] For example, Hall wrote on 1 Kings 17:3-6: 'O the strange caterers for Elijah! I know not whether it has been more miraculous, to preserve him without meat, or to provide meat by such mouths.' Matthew Henry picks up on this comment when writing of the ravens and calling them 'caterers'. Both father, Philip, and son, Matthew, were well acquainted with the poetry of George Herbert and used it in their writing.

While no evidence exists that he knew Aramaic and Syriac, yet from time to time he cites them when dealing with difficult Hebrew expressions. Thus, in writing on Isaiah 66:2 and the phrase, 'to him who is humble' ('el 'oni), he draws attention to the Syriac rendering, 'to him *that is quiet*', and the Chaldee (Aramaic), 'to him *that is meek*'. Probably he was drawing on the work of Dr John Lightfoot (1602-1675).[17]

Even before he started on his *Exposition*, Matthew Henry was in the habit of writing on Scripture. He also drew attention to this fact in his preface:

> It has long been my practice, what little time I had to spare in my study, from my constant preparations for the pulpit, to

---

16 Joseph Hall, *Contemplations on the Historical Passages of the Old and New Testaments* (London: Nath. Butter, 1626).

17 Lightfoot was Vice-Chancellor of the University of Cambridge, a member of the Westminster Assembly, and a scholar who devoted much time and effort to the Old Testament. His best known work, *Horae Hebraicae et Talmudicae*, was published in six volumes (1658-1678), some posthumously.

spend it drawing up expositions upon some parts of the New Testament, not so much for my own use, as purely for my own entertainment, because I knew not how to employ my thoughts, and time more to my satisfaction.[18]

In December 1700 he sent some of these expositions to his friend, Rev. Samuel Clark, with the following sentences regarding it:

> I leave it [the publishing] to you, and resolve to follow Providence, having often reflected with most comfort upon that which has been least my own doings. The work has been, and still is, to me its own wages, and the pleasure recompense enough for all the pains. You will please let me know, as there is occasion, what is done concerning them; if they return to the place from whence they came, they shall be heartily welcome. I shall not repent my writing of them, and I hope you will not repent the reading of them though they go no further.[19]

It is not clear why there was no progress on publication of it for another four years. On 12 November 1704 he began to write his notes on the Old Testament, which he completed on 18 July 1712. Then he worked on the New Testament, reaching the end of Acts on 17 April 1714. He was not spared to write any further, and others took over the task. They based their work on notes he had made, including almost complete ones on the Epistle to the Romans. He left some brief jottings on other epistles and there were also some shorthand notes of public and private expositions.[20] In all, four volumes appeared during his lifetime, starting with the Pentateuch in 1706, while he had just completed volume 5 before his death on 22 June 1714.

---

18 *Matthew Henry's Commentary*, vol. 1, p. ci.

19 Williams, *Memoirs*, p. 302.

20 For a list of those who completed the exposition of the New Testament, see Williams, *Memoirs*, p. 308.

There is a definite connection between Matthew Henry's commentary and his pastoral ministry. From the outset he lectured twice every Sunday to his congregation, and the content of many passages covered in his exposition was based on the sermons. If comparison is made between his sermons and his exposition of a particular text, the relationship can be seen very quickly. Here are just three examples, with the corresponding wording being underlined.

The first example comes from a sermon on Isaiah 55:3 (latter part) preached on 26 June 1692: 'And I will make an everlasting covenant with you, even the sure mercies of David.' These are some of the things he wrote:

2. that this covenant is an *everlasting* covenant. The contrivance of it was from everlasting. The continuance of it [is] everlasting. ...

3. the benefits of this covenant are *mercies*. They flow from God's mercy and are ordered hugely in kindness to us ....

4. they are *the mercies of David*, i.e. such mercies as God promised to David ....

5. they are *sure* mercies. The covenant of grace is sure. In the general purpose 'tis sure, i.e. God is real and sincere in the offer, serious and earnest, he is not a man, he's Jehovah (Exod. 6:3, 4, 6).

This is how the same material appears in his commentary on Isaiah 55:3:

Secondly, God's covenant with us is an everlasting covenant – its contrivance from everlasting, its continuance everlasting....

Thirdly, The benefits of this covenant are mercies suited to our case, who, being miserable, are the proper objects of mercy. They come from God's mercy, and are ordered every way in kindness to us.

Fourthly, They are the mercies of David, *such mercies as God promised to David* (Ps. lxxxxix, 28, 29 etc.) *which are called the mercies of David his servant....*

Fifthly, they are sure mercies. The covenant, being well-ordered in all things is sure. It is sure in the general purpose of it; God is real and sincere, serious and in earnest, in the offer of these mercies.

Another example can be taken from Psalm 89:30-33, giving first the words from a sermon preached on 8 May 1692:

1.   Affliction to true believers is but *a rod—visit their transgressions with the rod*—a rod not an axe, not a sword—for correction, not for destruction.... Gentleness in the affliction....

2.   It is a rod in the hand of God—I will visit, I that am in covenant with them. As this sweetens creature comforts yet they are God's sending so it sweetens crosses likewise and makes them easy, yet they come from his hand.

3.2   Not withstanding these afflictions—nevertheless—though David's seed be chastened yet it doth not follow that they are disinherited—though cast down yet not cast off—perplexed but not in despair (2 Cor. 4:8, 9).

In the *Exposition* they appear in this form:

But observe what affliction is to God's people.

1.   It is but a rod, not an axe, not a sword; it is for correction not for destruction. This denotes gentleness in affliction; it is the rod of men, such a rod as men use in correcting their children; and it denotes a design of good in and by the affliction, such a rod as yields the peaceable fruits of righteousness....

[2] The continuance of Christ's kingdom is made certain by the inviolable promise and oath of God, *notwithstanding all this* (v. 33).

1. It is a rod in the hand of God (I will visit them), he who is wise and knows what he does, gracious, and will do what is best....

Note, Afflictions are not only consistent with covenant-love, but to the people of God they flow from it. Though David's seed be chastened, it does not follow that they are disinherited; they may be cast down, but they are not cast off.

The final example relates to John 14:27. This is how he preached on it in January 1692:

> When our Lord Jesus was about to leave the world he made his will. His soul he committed to the hands of his Father (Luk. 23.46). His body he bequeathed to Joseph of Arimathea to be decently interred, yet not so as to see corruption. His clothes fell to the soldiers that crucified him (Luk. 23.34). His mother he left to the care of the beloved disciple (Joh. 19.26). But what should he bequeathe to his poor disciples, who had forsaken all to follow him? Silver and gold he had none to leave them, but he left them that which was infinitely better than thousands of gold and silver.[21]

This is how the same material appears in his commentary:

> When Christ was about to leave the world he *made his will*. His soul he committed to his Father; his body he bequeathed to Joseph, to be decently interred; his clothes fell to the soldiers; his mother he left to the care of John; but what should he leave to his poor disciples, that had left all for him? Silver and gold he had none; but he left them that which was infinitely better, his peace. '*I leave you*, but I leave *my peace* with you. I not only give you a title to it, but put you in possession of it'.[22]

Many more examples of this nature can be found when his sermons and commentary are examined. It is clear that he used previous compositions from his hand as he set about the task of writing a continuous commentary on the biblical text.

In 1704 he set himself to begin on an exposition of the whole of the Bible. He preached a funeral sermon for Rev. James Owen in 1706, and when it was published an advertisement was prefixed to it:[23] 'There is now in the press, and will shortly

---

21 Allan M. Harman, ed., *The Unpublished Sermons of Matthew Henry on the Covenant of Grace*, p. 77.

22 *Matthew Henry's Commentary*, vol. 5, p. 903.

23 The sermon, but not the advertisement, is reprinted in Matthew Henry's *Complete Works*, vol. II, pp. 527-47.

be published, an Exposition, with Practical Observations, on the Five Books of Moses, by the same author.' That was the commencement of a publication history of the exposition that continues to the present.

His industrious nature was already clear from his ministry up to 1704, but his diary reveals how steadily he worked on his *Exposition*. It was practically a daily occupation for the last ten years of his life, and accomplished amidst all the other pressures on his time. He was preparing the second volume when his eighth daughter, Theodosia, was born. With his wife in labour, he went to his study to carry on his work. His diary note was:

> Between two and three o'clock this morning, while my wife was ill [!], I retired to my study to seek God for her, and my children. Being willing to redeem time, I did a little at my Exposition; and Ezra 3 to the latter end, was before me, of the mixture of joy and sorrow; showing that the remembrance of former troubles ought not to drown the thankful sense of present mercies.[24]

Without all his previous experience and note-taking as an expositor, he could not possibly have kept up the demanding schedule. Here are some extracts from his diary that show the progress he made:

> Nov. 12 [1704] This night, after many thoughts of heart, and many prayers concerning it, I began my Notes on the Old Testament. It is not likely I should live to finish it, or if I should, that it should be of publick service, for I am not *par negotio*;[25] yet in the strength of God, and I hope with a single eye to his glory, I set about it; that I may endeavour something, and spend my time to some good purpose; and let the Lord make what use he pleaseth of me. I go about it with fear and trembling, lest I exercise myself in things too high for me, &c. The Lord help me to set about it with great humility.

---

24   Quoted in Williams, *Memoirs*, p. 177.

25   Latin, 'equal to the task'.

Jan 17, 1705. Studied in Gen. xiv.

July 19. Through the good hand of my God upon me, I finished Genesis. The Lord still go with me.

22. I began Exodus.

September 14. Studied in Exodus xxi. I am now come to the less pleasant part of the Mosaick writings; but thanks be to God *all* Scripture is profitable.

November 7. I finished Exodus, and entered on Leviticus.

30. Leviticus xvi. O that I may find Christ in the Old Testament, and may be led into the mystery of godliness. God was manifested by degrees.

December 7. Finished Leviticus xix. The Lord make me learned in his laws.

December 26. Leviticus xxvii.

28. Began Numbers.

December 31. I have pleasure in my study; for which I praise my God. Having obtained help from him I go on with much comfort to myself in my Notes on the Pentateuch. Whether ever they will be of use to any other and be accepted, He only knows who knows the hearts of all the children of men.

1705-6. January 2. Wrote Numbers ii, for a specimen of my Exposition and sent it to Mr Parkhurst, he desiring it, that if anything be amiss in the model I may be advertised of it.

15. Numbers viii. and ix. Mr Parkhurst writes to me that he will undertake the printing of the Exposition of the Pentateuch. The Lord direct in it.

March 8. Numbers 24. I had letters from the booksellers, and my friends at London, to urge me to send up what I have done of the Pentateuch.

On 10 March 1705, the Lord's Day, he began to read over his Notes from Genesis to Leviticus, and by 18 March he had completed this review. Then he resumed his work on the other two books of the Pentateuch, Numbers and Deuteronomy, completing them on 18 August 1706. He noted in his diary that it had been a year and nine months since he began his task. He added: 'Blessed be God who has helped me. I have written it with a great deal of pleasure, but my thoughts of publishing it have been with fear and trembling.' It was not until December of that year that he had confirmation that Mr Parkhouse in London would proceed with the publication of the volume on the Pentateuch.

By 9 September 1706 he had some of the proof pages on which he had to mark the errors, and he found more than printers' mistakes, for he wrote: 'I have reason to be ashamed of my own errata.' He also had to prepare a preface and sent it off on 2 October. On 12 November he received the last of the proofs, and was surprised to find prefixed to his annotations a commendatory letter by his friends, Revs John Shower and William Tong, about which he knew nothing until that moment. On 21 November he received a parcel of the printed copies and his diary insert was: 'I desire to bless God that he has given me to see it finished. I had comfort from that promise—Thou shalt find favour and good understanding in the sight of God and man.' At the end of the year, as always, he inserted a comment regarding the work of the past months. In reviewing 1706 he wrote:

> I who am unworthy to be employed by God at all, have been enabled by his free grace, to finish and publish, this year, the Exposition of the Pentateuch, with some hope of its being serviceable to the church of God. The glory of which I desire to give entirely to God. I have nothing to boast of.

The second volume, covering Joshua to Esther, took from 4 October 1706 until 20 May 1708. He had no break from the task, for on 1 June he started the third volume, covering Job, Psalms, Proverbs, Ecclesiastes and the Song of Solomon, and completed it by 16 February 1710.

Encouragement in his work came in various ways. While he was working on the third volume, he received a letter from a correspondent whom he did not know. From Exeter, Mr Samuel Bere wrote to him, acknowledging the benefit he had got from the *Exposition*. It is significant that he received this letter while in London, and considered this an encouragement that he should continue there, adding: 'For what reason have I to think that I should be more useful than I am, when God has been pleased to make me so much more useful than I am worthy to be.'

There was a short gap of two months in his work before he began the fourth volume on 11 April 1710. On the last day of the year he recorded his thanks to God for His mercy to him throughout it, and for the fact that he was able to bring out the third volume of the *Exposition* and also *The Method of Prayer*. On the following day, 1 January 1711, he asks that he:

> may write nothing that is frivolous, or foreign, or foolish, or flat, that I may give just Offence, or lead into any Mistakes; but that all may be clear, and pertinent, and affecting; that I may find out genuine Expositions; useful Observations; profitable Matter; and acceptable Words; if it shall please God to spare me to go on with it.[26]

At times he reached sections of text to which other commentators had come and those passages marked the end of their commentaries. For example, when writing on 2 Kings 11 to v. 16, he records that it was just here that Peter Martyr 'was in his learned Expositions when he fell sick and died'. When he got to Ezekiel 21 he commented that 'the excellent Calvin died at the end of his expounding Ezekiel 20'. He had to press on with his writing even when other things may have intruded into his task. On a visit to Hackney and the congregation he was to later serve (1712-14), he recorded that he should have been at a funeral but 'willing to read over the *Exposition* I had written

---

26   Tong, *Life of Matthew Henry*, p. 331.

here [while at Hackney], that I might leave them behind me, I stayed at home'.

His final volume was commenced just after he had moved to Hackney in May 1712. His full diary no longer exists for this period of his life. He was very occupied with preaching and lecturing, but yet he managed to keep up regular work on his *Exposition*. In accepting the call to Hackney he gave as one of his reasons that he would be near the printer, have access to books, and also profit from being in the company of learned scholars.[27] These expectations must have been realised. Here are some excerpts from his diary for this period of his ministry:[28]

1712. September 9. Began Matthew, but went in the morning to Salters' Hall, and stayed in town all day.

1713. February 10. Finished Matthew.

11. Began Mark.

March 21. Mark xvi. Began Luke.

July 10. Finished Luke. Began John.

November 27. John xxi. Finished John today. *Laus Deo* [Praise to God].

28. Began to read over the Gospels.

December 7. Read over John i. to vii.

11. Finished John.

Vol. VI. 1713. December 12. Began Acts, having first made an errand to the throne of grace for assistance.

1714. April 17. Finished Acts, and with it the 5th volume. Blessed be God that has helped me, and spared me. All the praise be to God.

19. Reviewed some of the sheets of the Acts.

April 21. Began the Preface, but did little in it.

---

27   See his reasons listed in chapter 8, p. 118.

28   These excerpts are found in Williams, *Memoirs*, p. 307.

23. Studied the Preface.

24. Went on in the Preface.

This work, done after he moved to Hackney, was in itself an amazing achievement. Starting in September 1712, by the end of December the following year he had finished the four Gospels and commenced Acts, which he completed on 24 April 1714, just prior to his final visit to Chester and his death while on the return journey.

Though he was not spared to write any further, others took over the task. They based their work on notes he had made, including almost complete ones on the Epistle to the Romans. He left some brief jottings on other epistles and there were also some shorthand notes of public and private expositions.[29] He had also given particular attention to the book of Revelation. Regarding this book and its message, Matthew Henry wrote about the views of other interpreters, including Dr Lightfoot and Rev. Richard Baxter, and said:

> I am far from taking them to be the best interpreters of the Apocalypse, and greatly prefer Durham;[30] when I have sometimes had occasion to expound the Revelation, with all tenderness to the application of it to particular events which I doubt not of its pointing to, I have attempted a *moral* or *practical* exposition of it; using it as a general key to God's providences concerning the church, and supposing by way of accommodation, that it hath many fulfillings, (as Hos. xi.).

3. The Nature of His Task as a Commentator
The intention in Matthew Henry's mind regarding his task is set out in the subtitle when the first volume was issued in 1706:[31]

---

29   For a list of those who completed the exposition of the New Testament, see Williams, *Memoirs*, p. 308.

30   His reference is to the Scottish theologian James Durham, *A Commentarie Upon the Book of Revelation* (Edinburgh: Christopher Higgins, 1658).

31   Two discussions I have found helpful are J. P. Thackway, 'Matthew

Wherein each chapter is summed up in its contents: The sacred text inserted at large in distinct paragraphs; each paragraph reduced to its proper heads; the sense given, and largely illustrated with practical remarks and observations.

In approaching Holy Scripture, Matthew Henry believed that we have to come to it recognising that it is indeed the Word of God, and treat it as such. 'Seriousness' or 'solemnity' has to be the characteristic that marks out our attitude to the text of the Bible. In writing about religion in the home he gave the instruction:

> Read the Scriptures to your families, in a solemn manner, requiring their attendance on your reading, and their attention to it; and inquiring sometimes whether they understand what you read. I hope you are none of you without Bibles in your houses, a store of Bibles, every one his Bible. Thanks be to God, we have them cheap and common in a language that we understand. The book of the law is not such a rarity with us as it was in Josiah's time. We need not fetch this knowledge from afar, nor send from sea to sea, and from the river to the ends of the earth, to see the word of God; no, the Word is near us....[32] It is better to be without bread in your houses than without Bibles, for the words of God's mouth are and should be to you more than any necessary food.[33]

In relation to the Old Testament, Matthew Henry encouraged his readers not to think of the Old Testament as 'an almanac out of date', but rather see it as is confirmed and illustrated in the New Testament. To read it aright, the Holy Spirit has to be the one who leads the reader into all truth.

Henry and His Commentary (Part 3)', *Bible League Quarterly* No. 378 (July-September, 1994), pp. 342-52, and Iain D. Campbell, 'Matthew Henry on the Aim of Exposition', *The Banner of Truth*, 383-4 (August-September, 1995), pp. 23-7.

32 This is an allusion to Deut. 30:11-14, words quoted by Paul in Rom. 10:6-8.

33 Matthew Henry, *Family Religion*, pp. 33-4.

This task of explaining the meaning of the biblical text he likens to removing the stone from the mouth of the well. Application, on the other hand, is like drawing the water out of the well. Not every verse of Scripture taught a practical lesson, but he considered it appropriate that he:

> endeavoured to mix with the exposition such hints or remarks as I thought profitable for doctrine, for reproof, for correction, for instruction in righteousness, aiming in all to promote practical godliness, and carefully avoiding the matters of doubtful disputation and strifes of words.[34]

The format of his comments is fourfold:

> *Preface.* Each volume of the *Exposition* has a preface, which sets out general reflections on the section of Scripture being addressed, with some indication of its structure and its general intent and purpose.

> *Introduction.* Each book of the Bible is introduced by a discussion that deals with the authorship and background, so that the reader of the commentary has that information as the text is approached.

> *Chapter Contents.* Each chapter of the exposition is preceded by a short summary, which outlines the contents and indicates the way in which the commentator is dealing with the text.

> *Exposition and Application.* The explanation is given in logical order, with heads and sub-heads. The sequence of enumeration is: I, 1., (1.), [1.], First. Points of application are inserted throughout the commentary, rather than being left to the end as is usual in his sermons (Use 1, Use 2, etc).

4. Conclusion

Why is Matthew Henry's work still so relevant? Several reasons can be given in answer to this question.

First, his commentary was not intended for academic theologians but for the ordinary people. Like his sermons, he was aiming at Christian believers who needed in print the same type of exposition

---

34   *Matthew Henry's Commentary*, vol. 1., p. cii.

as Matthew Henry gave to his congregations at Chester and Hackney. It was pulpit ministry given a new and lasting form in print.

Secondly, he set out in typical Reformation/Puritan style to deal directly with the text of Scripture. His primary interest is not in what others had written about the Bible, but rather his own view on the meaning and implications of Holy Scripture. He aimed to give his understanding of the text, and then some suggestions as to the practical outcome of accepting that meaning.

Thirdly, he wrote the commentary in the process of preaching, and therefore there is a pastoral touch to it. This sets it apart from many other commentaries. Just as his preaching ministry was coupled with prayer for divine help, so also his commentary was accompanied with petitions for help in its preparation and blessing in its use. It is a model of spiritual practicality. The content of the commentary was to produce spiritual change.

Fourthly, the *Exposition* has also been so effective because of the Puritan orderliness of exposition and preaching. This is what Joseph Pipa Jr. calls the 'logicality' of Puritan preaching. This is how he describes it:

> They began their sermons with a contextual introduction and a fairly brief exegetical discussion of the verse or verses with which they are dealing, explaining the terms and any particular grammatical construct that were important to the understanding of the text. Next they derived a doctrine from the text. That doctrine is not dissimilar from what we call a sermon proposition: a one-sentence summary of the truth taught in that text. Then they would offer a few proofs, primarily drawn from Scripture to support the truth derived from the text. Once the doctrine was confirmed they would then apply it in what they called 'uses'. Sometimes they would derive only one doctrine from a text, but other times they would derive two or three. In each instance, they would develop the doctrine with its proofs and uses before proceeding to the next doctrine.[35]

---

35 Joseph Pipa, 'Puritan Preaching', in Peter Lillback, ed., *The Practical Calvinist: An Introduction to the Presbyterian and Reformed Heritage* (Fearn: Christian Focus, 2002), pp. 169-70.

Fifthly, his commentary does not suffer from the prolixity of many of the Puritans.[36] Many of the Puritans wrote in a verbose style that was, and is, unnecessary. The Scottish commissioners to the Westminster Assembly commented on the length of the speeches and debates.[37] At the end of his life Richard Baxter wrote: 'And concerning almost all my writings I must confess that my own judgment is that fewer well studied and polished had been better.'[38] It is possible, too, that as a result of the ejection of 1662, many of the Puritans had time to give to their writings and hence they published far longer biblical expositions than if they had been occupied with parish commitments.

Sixthly, because of its evident spirituality it has appealed to successive generations of Christians. Accurate comments on the text are set in a context of new life in and through Christ. In itself it is recognition of the need of divine enlightenment if we are to understand Scripture aright. Those whose hearts have been warmed by gospel truth have an affinity with the comments of a spiritual pastor and writer.

As a final summary statement of the quality of Matthew Henry's *Exposition* and its continued value, let J. I. Packer have the last say:

> Simple and practical in style while thoroughly scholarly and well-informed for substance, the Commentary remains an all-time classic, standing head and shoulders above any other popular exposition produced either before or since.[39]

---

36 See the discussion by Leland Ryken, *Worldly Saints: The Puritans as They Really Were*, pp. 187-221 for comment on the faults of the Puritans, including their verbosity.

37 Robert Baillie, *Letters and Journals*, ed. David Laing (Edinburgh: Robert Ogle, 1841-2), vol. II, pp. 107-10, 120, 164, 177.

38 Richard Baxter, *Autobiography of Richard Baxter* (London: James Dent, 1931), p. 131.

39 Matthew Henry, *The Pleasantness of a Religious Life: A Puritan's View of the Good Life*, introduction by J. I. Packer (Fearn: Christian Heritage, 1998), p. 13.

CHAPTER 13

Other Writings

It is surprising that, in the midst of a very busy ministry, Matthew Henry was able to write so much. However, he was clearly very disciplined in his work, and made use of regular hours in his study as well as snatched moments to write a variety of work that was published either in his lifetime or later.[1]

He began with an address that was published anonymously in 1690. The original date of delivery is unknown, as were his reasons for not attaching his name to it. It was entitled 'A Brief Enquiry into the True Nature of Schism: or a Persuasive to Christian Love and Charity'.[2] It is clear in it that he was defending the right of the dissenters to absent themselves from worship in Anglican churches, and his desire for anonymity may well have been because of the bitterness of some against him at a local level. He pointed out that this is essentially a question that the New Testament, not the Old Testament, must answer. After surveying the use of the Greek word *schisma* in the New Testament, he indicated that the occurrences point to a division or break in fellowship, and this led to his definition of schism:

---

1   A chronological list of his writings can be found in *The Complete Works*, vol. I, p. ix.

2   The address can be found in *The Complete Works*, vol. II, pp. 353-61.

'Schism is an uncharitable distance, division, or alienation of affection among those who are called Christians, and agree in the fundamentals of religion, occasioned by their different apprehension about little things.'[3]

He described some of the practices that he regarded as schismatic, such as judging others, or separating from them on the basis of small differences, or separation from communion with those we have joined. Separation from parish churches to atheism or irreligion was wrong, as were the actions of those who condemned the parish churches as not being part of the visible church. Writing as a minister, Matthew Henry defended his right to preach and administer the sacraments outside the parish system.

> So, if I be a minister, and as such obliged to preach the gospel, yet kept out from the public exercise of my ministry by such terms and conditions, oaths and subscriptions, as I judge sinful; in such a case surely it is lawful for me, with Eldad and Medad,[4] to prophesy in the camp, since in my judgment the door of the tabernacle is made narrower than my Master has appointed it to be made. What should hinder but that as a minister of Christ, I may administer all the ordinances, according to Christ's institution, to those who are willing to join with me, and put themselves under my conduct (such as it is) in those administrations?[5]

What he wanted was that the sermons both within and without the parish churches 'promote, and propagate the gospel of peace, and by our prayers to prevail with God for a more plentiful pouring out of the Spirit of peace'. If this were to happen, he wrote,

> ... then I doubt not but that we should soon see our English Jerusalem established a praise in the midst of the earth.

---

3   Ibid., p. 356.

4   The reference is to Numbers 11:26-30.

5   *The Complete Works*, pp. 359-60.

And yet I am afraid even saints will be men; there will be remainders even of those corruptions which are the seed of schism, in the best, till we all come to the perfect man.

And that is the comfort of my soul, that if we can but once get to heaven, we shall be for ever out of the noise and hurry of this quarrelsome, contentious, dividing world, and the church triumphant shall be no more militant, but that happy world of everlasting light will be a world of everlasting love.[6]

He ended with an appeal that those who had been hating one another should now strive to love one another. The comfort he had was that in heaven he would be out of the 'quarrelsome, contentious, dividing world' when 'the church triumphant shall be no more militant, but that happy world of everlasting light will be a world of everlasting love'.

It was his friend William Tong who persuaded him to publish it, and who, when two opposing pamphlets appeared, went into press twice to defend him. The Rev. William Turner, vicar of Walburton, referred to Tong's response in a letter to Philip Henry. He wrote: 'Your son's book is orthodox, in my opinion; and agreeable to my rule of faith and charity; and his vindicator is a man of a brisk brain, and a sharp-nibbed pen.'[7] This reference is important as it clearly indicates that Matthew Henry was known as the author of the original pamphlet, and also suggests that William Tong was not as gentle in argumentation. Matthew Henry acknowledged to his father that sometimes he was tempted to use the same reproachful language as did his opponents. Getting over it was not easy, he wrote, but asked for his father's prayers that he might be confirmed in the work of the Lord.[8]

While his *Collection of Family Hymns* was published in 1694, Matthew Henry's next writing project was quite different from

---

6   Ibid., p. 361.

7   Williams, *Memoirs*, p. 223.

8   Ibid.

what he had done previously, and much more demanding. When his father Philip Henry died in 1696, he wanted Rev. James Owen to write a memoir, but he thought it best if Matthew Henry did it himself. There was a consensus among many who knew Philip Henry that an account of his life should 'conduce much to the glory of God's grace, and to the edification of many, especially of those that were acquainted with him'.[9] So Matthew Henry, amidst the demanding work of his pastorate, set about writing his father's biography, but not because Philip Henry was a public figure, for men hardly knew that he existed. The aim was not to advance the cause of any particular group but to set out the life of one who was so 'blameless, and harmless, and without rebuke'. Matthew was able to draw upon his father's extensive diaries and letters, quoting them widely as the best way to truly depict the life of one whose conduct showed him to be a man of 'sincere piety and devotedness to God'.

The book was published in 1698, and then a corrected reprint came out the following year. This edition was sold out, and just before he left Chester to go to Hackney, Matthew Henry brought out another edition in February 1712. In a Postscript to this edition, he noted that the book had often been sought by people who had found it very serviceable 'both for direction, quickening, and encouragement in the ways of God and godliness'.[10] His closing words in that Postscript are very self-depreciatory. He refers to his actions in publishing his father's life as 'troubling the world with the little affairs of my poor family'. However, he ends it by saying: 'I design nothing in it but, if it may be, by the grace of God, to do good to plain people like myself.'[11]

An abridged edition of the biography was brought out in 1765 by Rev. Job Orton, while Sir J. B. Williams had the

---

9   From Matthew Henry's preface to the first edition of *The Life of the Rev. Philip Henry*, p. xxxvii.

10   Ibid., p. xli.

11   Ibid., p. xliii.

advantage of handwritten material, especially Philip Henry's diaries, as he worked on the edition that was published in 1825. It does not appear to have been republished until the Banner of Truth Trust did so in 1974.

Many later Christians were blessed by reading this biography. John Wesley, in his journal for 7-15 November 1741, recorded that he had that day read some of Turretin's *History of the Church* ('a dry, heavy, barren treatise', wrote Wesley) but also 'the Life of that truly good and great man, Mr Philip Henry'.[12] Another who appreciated it was the Scot, Dr Thomas Chalmers, leader and first moderator of the Free Church of Scotland at the time of the Disruption of 1843. He said that it was 'one of the most precious religious biographies in our language'.[13]

In catechising Matthew Henry used the Westminster *Shorter Catechism,* but found that for the younger children something with more explanation was needed.[14] He did not intend it to be as extensive as it became, but believed that because he broke each answer into several short questions it was more manageable for children. At first he appended questions which had to be answered by 'Yes' or 'No', but later he attached a Scripture verse for every answer. In addition, in framing the questions, he was trying to press home to children spiritual matters and make them realise that the truths of Scripture were to be their personal concern. This was first published in 1703, and it went through three editions during his lifetime.[15] Here is an illustration of his method:

---

12 *The Works of John Wesley*, 3rd edn. (Grand Rapids: Baker Book House, 1991), vol. I, p. 347.

13 Thomas Chalmers, *Endowments.*

14 For a general discussion of catechisms in this period, see J. Lewis Wilson, 'Catechisms and the Puritans', *Puritan Papers*, ed. J. I. Packer (Phillipsburg: Presbyterian & Reformed, 2004), vol. 4 1965-7, pp. 137-54.

15 *A Scripture Catechism, in the Method of the Assembly's, The Complete Works,* vol. II, pp. 174–263.

Q. 6 *Are there more gods than one?*

A. There is but one only, the living and true God.

1. Are there many gods? No: for though there be that are called gods, yet there is but one God, I Cor. viii.5, 6. Can there be any but one? No; for he had said, I am God, and there is none else; I am God, and there is none like me, Isa. xlvi.9. Are you sure there is but one? Yes: for the Lord our God is one Lord and there is none other but he, Mark xii. 29, 32.

2. Is the God whom we serve that one God? Yes: for Jehovah he is God, Jehovah he is God, I Kings xviii.39. Is he infinitely above all pretenders? Yes: for he is a great King above all gods, Ps. xcv.3. Is he God alone? Yes: O Lord of hosts, God of Israel, thou art the God, even thou alone, Isa. xxxvii.16. Are all other gods false gods? Yes: for all the gods of the nations are idols, but the Lord made the heavens, Ps. xcvi.5.

3. Is our God the true God? Yes: the Lord he is the true God, Jer. x.10. Is he the only true God? Yes: this is life eternal, to know the only true God, John xvii.3. Is he the living God? Yes: the living God, and an everlasting King, Jer. x.10. Is he the Sovereign Lord? Yes: for he is God over all, blessed for evermore, Rom. ix.5. Is this one God enough? Yes: for he is God All-Sufficient, Gen. xvii.1.[16]

4. Is the Lord Jehovah the maker of all things? Yes: he is the everlasting God, even the Lord, the Creator of the ends of the earth, Isa. xl.28. Is he your Maker? Yes: he is the Lord our Maker, Ps. xcv.6. Is he the owner of all things? Yes: for he is the most high God, possessor of heaven and earth, Gen. xiv.19. Is he your rightful owner? Yes: we are the people of his pasture, and the sheep of his hand, Ps. xcv.7. Is he the ruler of all things? Yes; for his kingdom ruleth over all, Ps. ciii.19. Is he your ruler? Yes: O Lord, truly I am thy servant, I am thy servant, Ps. cxvi.16. Is he the benefactor of all the creatures? Yes: for he giveth to all life, and breath, and all things, Acts xvii.25.

---

16   Here Matthew Henry is referring to the Hebrew text that says that God identified himself as *El Shaddai*, which, according to one derivation, means God All-Sufficient.

Is he your benefactor? Yes: for he daily loadeth us with his benefits, Ps. lxviii.19. Shall he therefore be yours by your own consent? Yes: O God, thou art my God, Ps. lxiii.1.

It is significant that after the formation of the Free Church of Scotland in 1843, when it embarked on a major publishing enterprise, the decision was made to reissue Matthew Henry's catechism.[17] Dr James Begg, of Newington Free Church in Edinburgh, wrote the foreword, in which he said:

> But whilst the name of its venerated author will probably secure for this republication a cordial reception amongst true Christians on both sides of the Tweed, the work itself will be found replete with all the solid sense, sound doctrine, enlarged spiritual discernment, and, above all, singular power in the felicitous application of Scripture, for which the Author of the Commentary was so remarkably distinguished.[18]

The next publication of Matthew Henry was *The Communicant's Companion: or Instructions and Helps for the right receiving of the Lord's Supper*. It was published in 1704, and immediately won acceptance as an impressive explanation of the Puritan view of the Lord's Supper.[19] Its enthusiastic reception seemed to take Matthew Henry by surprise for he wrote in his diary:

> I desire, with all humility, to give God praise for what acceptance my book on the sacrament has met with; the intimations I have had thereof from divers, I desire may never be the matter of my pride, (the Lord mortify that in me) but ever, ever the matter of my praise.[20]

---

17 *An Exposition of the Shorter Catechism, or, A 'Scripture Catechism in the Method of the Assembly's':* Issued by Authority of the Publication Committee of the General Assembly of the Free Church of Scotland (Edinburgh: John Lowe, 1847).

18 Ibid., p. 3.

19 Horton Davies, *The Worship of the English Puritans*, p. 212, expresses the view that it is 'the most complete statement of the Puritan doctrine of the Lord's Supper'.

20 Matthew Henry's Diary, quoted in Williams, *Memoirs*, p. 226.

As he set out the doctrine of the Lord's Supper, he reverted to his oft-repeated practice of using alliterative headings to summarise his views: [The Lord's Supper] 'was appointed to be a commemorating Ordinance, and a confessing Ordinance; a communicating Ordinance, and a covenanting Ordinance'. He expressed the general Puritan view that it was not just a bare sign but an ordinance in which Christ's benefits are communicated to believers:

> Christ, and all his benefits, are here communicated to us. Here is not only bread and wine set before us to be looked at, but given to us to be eaten and drank; not only Christ made known to us, that we may contemplate the mysteries of redemption, but Christ made over to us, that we may participate of the benefits of redemption. God, in this ordinance, not only assures us of the truth of the promise, but according to our present case and capacity, conveys to us by his Spirit the good things promised.[21]

In 1710 Matthew Henry published a short life of Lieutenant Richard Illidge.[22] Even though no author was given, his diary made it plain that it was from his pen. As the title indicated, the majority of this little work was in Illidge's own words, so that his 'thoughts, expressions, prayers, and self-reflections, may suit the case of many others'.[23] Illidge was converted at the age of 57, and then started to record in writing his religious experiences until he died in 1709 at the age of seventy-two. His journal is another indication of the spirituality of Christians in that period.

One of Matthew Henry's most influential publications is *A Method of Prayer*, written while he was still at Chester and

---

21   *The Complete Works*, vol. I, pp. 294-5.

22   'A Concise Account of the Life of Lieutenant Illidge, Fifty Years in the Militia of the County of Chester: Chiefly Collected from His Own Papers', *The Complete Works*, vol. II, pp. 553-86.

23   Ibid., p. 553.

published in 1710.[24] It, along with Isaac Watts' *A Guide to Prayer*,[25] shows a concern that prayer would not be disfigured by 'infelicity of phraseology and disordered rambling'.[26] Between finishing his third volume of the *Exposition* and starting the fourth, he turned his hand to the preparation of a manual to guide Christians. This is what he said in his preface:

> ... I was willing to take a little time from that work to this poor performance, in hopes that it might be of some service to the generation of them that seek God, that seek the face of the God of *Jacob*: And if any good Christians receive assistance from it in their devotions, I hope they will not deny me one request, which is, that they will pray for me, that I may obtain mercy of the Lord to be found among the faithful watchmen of *Jerusalem's* walls, who never hold their peace day or night, but give themselves to the word and prayer, that at length I may finish my course with joy.[27]

He recognised that many other aspects of prayer could be added, and suggested that an interleaved book would be a valuable aid so that other headings could be inserted. Other books were already available on prayer, but Matthew Henry believed that few Christians were going to complain about another one from which they could get help. He was a prayerful pastor, and his

---

24 It has been reprinted many times. The best edition is the one edited by J. Ligon Duncan III, Matthew Henry, *A Method of Prayer: Freedom in the Face of God* (Fearn: Christian Heritage, 2001). The advantage of this edition is that it was produced after study of the various editions and makes the necessary corrections. See also the discussion by H. O. Old, 'Matthew Henry and the Puritan Discipline of Family Prayer', pp. 77-82.

25 Isaac Watts, *A Guide to Prayer* (Edinburgh: Banner of Truth Trust, 2001). This book was first published in 1715, the year after Matthew Henry's death.

26 These expressions are those of Horton Davies, *The Worship of the English Puritans*, p. 113. His chapter on 'Puritan Prayer-Books' (pp. 115-61) discusses the historical background to the books on prayer of Henry and Watts.

27 Ibid., pp. 16-17.

suggestions are suitable for individuals or for those who lead in public prayer.

Among the forms of prayer he included are some to be used by children. Here are some petitions from this section:

> Thou madest me for thyself, to show forth thy praise.
> But I am a sinner; I was shapen in iniquity, and in sin did my mother conceive me.
> God be merciful to me a sinner.
> O deliver me from the wrath to come, through Jesus, who died for me and rose again.
> Lord, give me a new nature. Let Jesus be formed in my soul, that to me to live may be Christ, and to die may be gain.[28]

This concern for children's religious life and expression is but another example of the way in which Matthew Henry tried to reach young people with the gospel. In addition to his catechising, carried out each Saturday afternoon, he preached sermons in which he addressed the children. Here is an example:

> Lay yourselves at Christ's feet, and he will take you up in his arms. Give yourselves to him, and he will give himself in his graces and comforts to you. Lie in his way, by a diligent attendance on his ordinances, and he will not pass by without putting his hand on you. And if you value his blessings aright, and be earnest with him for blessings, he will bless you with the best of blessings, such as will make you eternally blessed.[29]

This book was followed by three sermons on prayer that he gave after he moved to Hackney, showing how a Christian may start, spend and close the day in prayer.[30] The sermons were delivered in late August and early September 1712, and in sending them out in printed form Matthew Henry had his

---

28   Ibid., p. 167.

29   *The Complete Works*, vol. II, p. 274; Matthew Henry, *Family Religion*, p. 117.

30   These are included in *A Method of Prayer: Freedom in the Face of God*, pp.199-285.

friends back in Chester in mind. This is what he said in the preface:

> I am not without hopes, that something may hereby be contributed among plain people, by the blessing of God upon the endeavour, and the working of his grace with it, to the promoting of serious godliness, which is the thing I aim at. And yet I confess I had not published it, but designing it for a present to my dearly beloved friends in the country, whom I have lately been rent from.[31]

The sermons were on three appropriate passages (Ps. 5:3, *My voice shalt thou hear in the morning, O Lord; in the morning will I direct my prayer unto thee, and will look up*; Ps. 25:5, *On thee do I wait all the day*; Ps. 4:8, *I will both lay me down in peace, and sleep: for thou Lord, only makest me dwell in safety*). He wanted to make the point that communion with God is essential if we are to grow in grace and become more fitted to share in the joy of heaven. All those who go to heaven begin their heaven now. The sermons were practical in their orientation, and called upon Christians to live lives dedicated to God and in humble dependence on His grace.

The final book that Matthew Henry prepared for the press was on the joys of the Christian life. Its title now seems strange, yet in the period in which it was published it would have been easily understood. The title was, *The Pleasantness of a Religious Life Opened and Improved; and Recommended to the Consideration of All, Particularly of Young People.* In the preface he tells his readers that he preached six sermons on this topic the previous year, and after requests he was making it available for the wider public. He wrote:

> [I] take this opportunity to prepare it for the press, when, through the good hand of God upon me, I have finished my fifth volume of expositions, before I go to the sixth. And herein, I confess, I indulge an inclination of my own; for this

---

31   *The Complete Works*, vol. I, p. 198.

doctrine of the pleasantness of religion is what I have long had a particular kindness for, and taken all occasions to mention. Yet I would not thus have gratified either my friends' requests, or my own inclination, if I had not thought that, by the blessing of God, it might be of some service to the common interest of Christ's kingdom, and the common salvation of precious souls.[32]

Modern readers have to understand that this book encompasses the Puritans' vision of the Christian life. They were not morbid and unfeeling. Rather, serving God was with them a thing of the highest joy. Matthew Henry expressed the Christian's pleasure in God as one 'which has no pain attending to it, no bitterness in the latter end of it; a pleasure which God himself invites you to, and which will make you happy, truly and eternally happy, and shall not this work for you?'[33]

Some other writings of Matthew Henry were only published after his death. It is uncertain when he started to think about baptism and write on it. However, in his diary he noted: '1707, August 15. I had a letter from a meeting of ministers in Buckinghamshire, to urge me to publish something of the baptismal covenant; the Lord direct my studies, and incline me to that in which he will own me.' This request may have been because of sermons that he preached on the sacraments in 1694-5, or because friends knew of his ability to state Christian truth precisely. However, what he prepared was never printed in his lifetime, but an abridgement by Thomas Robins appeared in 1783. The Rev. S. Palmer, in his account of Matthew Henry's life prefixed to the 1811 edition of his commentary, said that he had compared it with the original and that the aim had been 'to retain everything important, and omit what was redundant'. It was published in

---

32   Ibid., p. 1; *The Pleasantness of a Religious Life: A Puritan's view of the Good Life*, introduction by J. I. Packer (Fearn: Christian Heritage, 1998), p. 20.

33   Ibid., p. 49.

his collected works,[34] and also recently in a collection of his writings on the Christian family.[35]

The doctrine of baptism that he explains is that of the Westminster Confession and Catechisms. Baptism is a sign and seal of God's covenant, but he strenuously opposes any promiscuous use of the sacrament. Children of unbelieving parents have to wait till they can ask for baptism themselves. 'Yet the children of parents, one of whom professes faith in Christ and obedience to him, have a right to baptism; the "unbelieving parent" is so far sanctified by the believing, that the children are "federally holy".'[36] He demonstrates that this view of baptism has no place for baptismal regeneration. Sacraments do not confer grace by the mere administration, but depend upon the blessing of God. His discussion concluded with directions to parents bringing their children for baptism and for those present who witnessed it.

Short biographical pieces concerning two of his sisters were written by Matthew Henry but not published until 1819 by J. B. Williams. Eleanor (Mrs Radford) and Ann (Mrs Hulton) died within three weeks of each other in August 1697. Drawing upon Eleanor's diaries and letters to her sisters, Matthew Henry penned a brief account of his sister. It was preserved in a copy in the handwriting of her oldest sister, Sarah (Mrs Savage).[37] A much longer biography of his sister Ann was also preserved in handwritten form by descendants until it was published in 1819. It was intended for the family, and though Matthew Henry was urged to publish it, he declined. The family tradition was that he 'deemed any attempt to increase the notoriety of his family inconsistent with modesty'.[38] Both these works show

---

34   *The Complete Works*, vol. I, pp. 489-566.

35   Matthew Henry, *Family Religion*, pp. 128-287.

36   Ibid., p. 170.

37   'Memoirs of Mrs Radford, by her brother the Reverend Matthew Henry', 4th ed., Appendix V, *Memoirs of the Life and Character of Mrs Sarah Savage*, pp. 264-76.

38   Ibid., p. 279

that the same spirituality apparent in Matthew Henry's own life was exhibited also in the lives of his sisters.

If Matthew Henry had completed five volumes of his *Exposition* during a busy pastorate, this would have been considered an amazing feat. But to publish so many other works as well points to a highly systematic pastor and scholar. By spoken *and* written word he was ministering not only to his own day but to successive generations of Christians who have been blessed by them. The continual printing of Matthew Henry's writings is testimony to their worth.

CHAPTER 14

The Impact of Matthew Henry

An examination of the catalogue of any major library in the English-speaking world soon reveals the number of works by Matthew Henry that it holds. These include the commentary in its various editions and his other writings.[1] It is apparent that from his own day to the present there has been a continuous stream of reprinting and adaptation of his work, including his 'gems' and sermon outlines taken from his commentary. I want to trace in particular some of his early influence, especially on Jonathan Edwards, John and Charles Wesley, and George Whitefield, before giving a brief overview of the later impact of his work.[2]

Books from Britain soon made their way across the Atlantic, and evidently Matthew Henry's *Exposition* and his other works became known and were used. Jonathan Edwards was one of those readers, not only of the *Exposition*, but also of his books *A Communicant's Companion* and *A Method of Prayer*. His father,

---

1   As I am writing in Australia, I checked the holdings on Matthew Henry in the Australian National Library in Canberra. It holds over 1,000 items by him.

2   For the Wesleys and Whitefield I have written a fuller discussion of them in 'The Impact of Matthew Henry's *Exposition* on 18th Century Christianity', *EQ* 82.1 (2010), 3-14. This article also has the fuller bibliographical information.

Timothy Edwards, pastor at East Windsor, Connecticut, owned both of these books, and in 1716/17 lent the former of these on two occasions. We know that Jonathan Edwards borrowed from someone else Matthew Henry's sermon delivered on the occasion of Mr Atkinson's ordination on 7 January 1713,[3] but more importantly that he had a set of Henry's commentaries. Much in Matthew Henry's *Exposition* was relevant for Jonathan Edwards, since they both were concerned not just with the close attention to the text of Scripture but also with its practical application.

The influence of Matthew Henry is patent in three places in Edwards's works, the 'Notes on Scripture'[4], his sermons and the 'Blank Bible'.[5] He commenced making notes on Scriptural passages at an early stage of his ministry, though it is unclear whether he ever contemplated writing a full commentary on the whole Bible. On most biblical books he wrote some notes, and thirteen direct quotes from Matthew Henry appear. In his sermons considerable use of Matthew Henry is evident. For example, when explaining Isaiah, Edwards relied very heavily on Henry, not only for the interpretation of individual passages but also for his understanding of the structure of the whole book.[6]

Much greater use of the *Exposition* was made in the 'Blank Bible'. This was a small copy of the Authorised Version with interleaved blank pages so that comments could be inserted. When his brother-in-law, Thomas Pierpont, gave up his intention to study for the ministry in 1730, he handed over this volume to Jonathan Edwards. Over the next three decades, Edwards made approximately 5,500 entries in what he paradoxically called his

---

3   This sermon is printed in *The Complete Works*, vol. II, pp. 496-511.

4   *The Works of Jonathan Edwards*, Vol. 15, ed. Stephen J. Stein (Yale: Yale University Press, 1998).

5   *The Works of Jonathan Edwards*, Vol. 24, ed. Stephen J. Stein (Yale: Yale University Press, 2006).

6   See the discussion by David Barshinger, '"The Only Rule of Faith and Practice": Jonathan Edwards's Interpretation of the Book of Isaiah as a Case Study of His Exegetical Boundaries', *JETS* 52:4 (December 2009), pp. 811-29.

'Blank Bible'. Matthew Henry is quoted 205 times in it, 204 in the Old Testament, and only once in the New Testament.[7]

Even a greater number of references to Matthew Poole's *Synopsis Criticorum aliorumque Scripturæ Interpretum* occurs (for it Edwards used the abbreviation *SSS*), though the references to Matthew Henry are normally fuller quotations. The next most-quoted source is Philip Doddridge's notes.[8] In Edwards's volume on the Apocalypse (the Book of Revelation)[9] he only cites Matthew Henry once (a quotation from his comments on Joshua 4:19, and another on Numbers 14:23-24). The modern editor of this work notes that the use made of Matthew Henry's *Exposition* in the 'Notes on Scripture' and the 'Blank Bible' suggests 'that this popular commentator was more influential upon his ideas and interpretation of the Bible than the infrequent use in the "Apocalypse" implies'.[10]

Turning to Britain, the Wesley brothers knew and appreciated the work of both Matthew Henry and his father, Philip Henry, who had been ejected from the Anglican parish of Worthenbury in Flintshire in 1662. John Wesley, even though he disagreed with Matthew Henry's Calvinism, yet recommended use of his *Exposition*. When he came to write his notes on the Old Testament, he felt he did not have the necessary learning and immediately thought of the *Exposition*. Here is his assessment of it:

---

7   No ready explanation can be given of why there is this discrepancy between the use of Matthew Henry in the Old Testament as over against the New Testament.

8   Philip Doddridge, *The Family Expositor*. A tabulation is provided by Stephen Stein showing the use made of Poole, Henry and Doddridge in Edwards's Blank Bible. What is notable is that Poole and Henry were used almost exclusively in the Old Testament (Poole, 778 times out of 782; Henry, 204 times out of 205), while Doddridge was used almost exclusively in the New Testament (297 times in the NT as over against 6 times in the OT). See *The Works of Jonathan Edwards*, Vol. 25 (Yale: Yale University Press, 2006), p. 60.

9   *The Works of Jonathan Edwards*, Vol. 5, ed. Stephen Stein (Yale: Yale University Press, 1977).

10   Ibid., p. 63.

He [Matthew Henry] is allowed by all competent judges to have been a person of strong understanding, of various learning, of solid piety, and much experience of the ways of God. And his exposition is generally clear and intelligible, the thoughts being expressed in *plain* words: It is also *sound*, agreeable to the tenor of Scripture, and to the analogy of faith. It is frequently *full*, giving a sufficient explication of the passages which require explaining. It is in many parts *deep*, penetrating further into the inspired writings than most other commentators do. It does not entertain us with vain speculations, but is practical throughout; and usually *spiritual* too, teaching us how to worship God, not in form only, but 'in spirit and in truth'.[11]

Another major difficulty that Wesley had with Henry's *Exposition* was the cost, as the set of six volumes was priced at six guineas (£6. 6. 0.). This amount was about one quarter of what a working man would earn in a year. In addition, hard-working people had little time to read the six large volumes. The solution, Wesley contended, was an abridgement, which would allow for omission of the parts to which he had theological objections. In the end he used Matthew Poole extensively and added notes culled from Henry. Wesley's *Notes on the Old Testament* did not sell well, and when he died in 1791 there were still 750 copies of it unsold.

It has often been noted that Charles Wesley's hymn 'A charge to keep I have, a God to glorify', is based on Matthew Henry's comment on Leviticus 8:35, and uses many of his phrases. This is how the commentary runs:

We have every one of us a charge to keep, an eternal God to glorify, an immortal soul to provide for, needful duty to be done, our generation to serve; and it must be our daily duty to keep this charge, for it is the charge of the Lord our Master, who will shortly call us to an account about it.

But the link is much closer than this isolated case might suggest. Charles Wesley himself drew attention to his dependence on Matthew Henry, Dr Gill on the Pentateuch, and Bengel on

---

11   Preface to *Explanatory Notes upon the Old Testament*, reprinted in *The Works of John Wesley*, vol. XIV, p. 247.

the New Testament.[12] Not surprisingly, many of his hymns are dependent on Matthew Henry.[13] Take, for example, this verse of his hymn based on Exodus 34:5-6:

> Its streams the whole creation reach,
> So plenteous is the store,
> Enough for all, enough for each,
> Enough for evermore.

Clearly this is based on Matthew Henry's comment on this passage: 'The springs of mercy are always full, the streams of mercy always flowing; there is mercy enough in God, enough for all, enough for each, enough for ever.'

The same is true of his two-stanza hymn,

> Captain of Israel's Host, and Guide
> of all that seek that land above,

which follows Matthew Henry's commentary on Exodus 13:21. In fact, Timothy Dudley-Smith has noted that there is correspondence in eleven out of the sixteen lines, 'often, but not always in identical words'.[14] All this means that Charles Wesley was deeply familiar with the *Exposition* and utilised it as a source of inspiration

---

12 In the preface to his *Short Hymns on Select Passages of Scripture* (1762), he noted that God had disabled him for the principal work of ministry, but given him the opportunity to write hymns, and then acknowledged his indebtedness to Henry, Gill and Bengel. The quotation can be found easiest in John R. Tyson, ed., *Charles Wesley: A Reader* (Oxford: Oxford University Press, 2000), p. 377.

13 The fullest discussion is A. Kingsley Lloyd, 'Charles Wesley's Debt to Matthew Henry', *London Quarterly and Holborn Review* (1946), pp. 330-7. See my discussion in 'The Impact of Matthew Henry's *Exposition* on 18th Century Christianity', 7-9. When I wrote I was unaware of another article dealing with the connection between Matthew Henry and Charles Wesley. This is by Erik Routley, 'Charles Wesley and Matthew Henry', *The Congregational Quarterly*, vol. XXXIII (1955), pp. 345-51. His conclusions are almost identical to mine, and he adds some further comparative examples.

14 Timothy Dudley-Smith, *A Flame of Love: A personal choice of Charles Wesley's verse* (London: Triangle, 1987), p. 92.

for his hymn writing. Probably this was made easier because of Matthew Henry's style that involved rhythmic phrases and memorable lines. When Wesley wanted to write a hymn based on a biblical passage, 'he turned first to Matthew Henry to see what ideas the venerable Puritan commentator was prepared to share with him'.[15] While Wesley drew on many sources, sacred and secular, yet for biblical exegesis he was heavily dependent on Henry.[16]

Just as the Wesley brothers knew and used Matthew Henry, so did George Whitefield. He was converted in Oxford but when back in Gloucester he lived over a bookshop run by George Harris. From him he obtained a copy of the *Exposition*. He could not pay at once but over a period of time he did so, and it became his lifetime companion. Often before preaching he retired by himself and used Samuel Clarke's *Bible* (a Puritan product, reprinted in 1759 with 'A Preface to the Serious Reader' by Whitefield), Matthew Henry's *Exposition* and Cruden's *Concordance*.

While the connection with Matthew Henry has often been observed,[17] little work has been done on examining Whitefield's sermons to ascertain how far they reflect Henry's *Exposition*. Care is needed in making judgments, for only sixty-three of Whitefield's sermons are extant, representing mainly the early period, before he was twenty-five years of age, and the closing years of his ministry. Many other printed sermons claimed to be Whitefield's, but he had to disown them. In his journal for October 1740 he wrote: 'I also met with two volumes of sermons published in London, supposed to have been delivered by me, though I have never preached on most of the texts.'[18]

---

15 Erik Routley, 'Charles Wesley and Matthew Henry', p. 345.

16 Erik Routley pointed out that a study of this relationship between Matthew Henry and Charles Wesley not only lets us see the obvious debt which Wesley owes to Henry, but also '(what is more precious) in perhaps sending some readers back to the great spiritual joys that wait for them in reading his Commentaries'. *Ibid.*, p. 351.

17 Cf. the comments of A. Dallimore, *George Whitefield: The Life and Times of the Great Evangelist of the Eighteenth-Century Revival* (Edinburgh: Banner of Truth Trust, 1970), vol. 1, pp. 82, 128; vol. 2, pp. 168, 481, 567.

18 George Whitefield, *Journal*, p. 484.

The best study of the link between Matthew Henry and Whitefield is by David Crump, who examined nine sermons, dating from 1736 to 1763.[19] The borrowing is certain, though Whitefield was no slavish imitator. He was well-read in Puritan theology, but was extremely conversant with Matthew Henry. This comes out in the way in which he used ideas from Henry's *Exposition* from biblical sections other than the one he was addressing. For example, when dealing with the new birth when preaching on 2 Corinthians 3:17, he drew upon Matthew Henry's commentary on John 3. When preaching on Romans 14:17 at Cambuslang (a town south-east of Glasgow) on Sunday evening, 13 September 1741, Whitefield drew heavily upon Henry's discussion on Romans 14:1-4. Crump's conclusion is that 'if the spontaneous Whitefield were using Henry as much as the prepared Whitefield it would say a great deal about the thoroughness with which Henry had been assimilated by the great preacher.'[20]

No figures can be produced to show how many copies of Matthew Henry's *Exposition* were actually sold or distributed in the eighteenth century. Consultation of the catalogues of the British Library, London, or the Bodleian Library, Oxford, shows that numerous reprints or editions of it were made right from the time the volume on the Pentateuch was first issued in 1706. A great variety of printers issued editions, and on some occasions one printer did so on behalf of himself and others. One such edition was printed for one man and thirteen other printers or booksellers. By the end of the eighteenth century the need for an abbreviated edition of the commentary was felt, and *The Beauties of Henry* came out in 1797.[21]

---

19 David Crump, 'The Preaching of George Whitefield and His Use of Matthew Henry's *Commentary*', *Crux*, XXV, 3 (September, 1989), pp. 19-28. In an appendix to his article (pp. 25-26) he provides outlines of two sermons (on Eccles. 4:9-12 and Luke 18:9-14), showing the verbal correspondences between Henry and Whitefield.

20 Ibid., p. 21.

21 *The Beauties of Henry: a selection of the most striking passages in the exposition of that celebrated commentator: To which is prefixed a brief account of the life, character, and death of the author* (London: John Geard, 1797).

Matthew Henry and his various writings became well-known in Scotland, though it does not appear that any edition of his *Exposition* was printed in Scotland. However, several of his shorter works were published in Edinburgh or Glasgow. For example, his sermon, 'A Church in the House: A Sermon concerning family religion', was reprinted in Edinburgh for James McEwen in 1714 and was 'to be sold at his house at the Head of Niddrie's Wynd'. When an edition of the metrical Psalms was issued in 1770, an analysis of the contents of each psalm was added, taken from Matthew Henry's *Exposition*.[22] This edition was so popular that another one was called for in 1783, and in particular the note on the title page is significant in that it indicates that the analysis of the Psalms is by Matthew Henry 'the biblical commentator'. Note was being taken of the significance of Matthew Henry for in John Brown's *The Christian, the student, the pastor*, Matthew Henry was one of his examples, along with men of the prominence of James Hogg and Thomas Halyburton in Scotland, John Owen and Philip Doddridge in England, and Cotton Mather and Jonathan Edwards in America.[23]

Extensive knowledge of his writings had developed in America by the mid-eighteenth century. The need for an abridged version of his commentary was met by a volume with extracts from his full *Exposition*, intended to meet the needs of those who could not purchase his larger commentary.[24] An American edition of the metrical psalter first published in

22 *The Psalms of David in metre: according to the version approved by the Church of Scotland. With an analysis or brief view of the contents of each Psalm, taken from the exposition of Mr Matthew Henry* (Edinburgh: Robert Clark, 1770).

23 John Brown, *The Christian, the student, and pastor, exemplified in the lives of Mess. James Frazer, James Hogg, Thomas Halyburton, in Scotland; Owen Stockton, Matthew Henry, Philip Doddridge, in England; Thomas Shepherd, Cotton Mather, and Jonathan Edwards, in America* (Edinburgh: G. Als[ton], 1781).

24 *Extracts from Mr Henry's annotations on the Bible. Published for the benefit of such as are not able to purchase his works at large* (Worcester, Mass.: Isaiah Thomas, 1775).

Scotland was printed in 1791,[25] with another edition coming very quickly in 1795. Another volume by Matthew Henry consisted of prayers, mainly in the language of Scripture. The title of this book again identifies the author as the author of the biblical commentary.[26]

By the early nineteenth century the demand for his *Exposition* was so great across the Atlantic that an American edition was prepared and issued in 1828. It had a lengthy introduction and assessment of Matthew Henry's work by Dr Archibald Alexander of Princeton.[27] He explained that he had long used it, and analysed its character that had made it so widely used. He described the two classes of commentaries, the critical and the practical, before going on to deal in greater detail with Henry's *Exposition*:

> The best helps ought, therefore, to be provided, to enable all classes of men to form correct opinions on the all-important subject of religion. For this reason, many practical expositions, not only of detached passages and single books, but of the whole Bible, have been composed, and have been extensively useful in elucidating the Scriptures; and in teaching how the truths of revelation may be applied to regulate the hearts and direct the lives of men. In this class, Henry's Exposition holds a distinguished place. This work has now been before the Christian community for more than a hundred years, and has, from its first publication, been so well received, and is so generally approved, that all recommendation of the work itself seems to be now superfluous.

---

25 It was printed and sold by Peter Stewart, no. 34 South Second-Street, Philadelphia.

26 *Prayers in Scripture Expressions: for the use of families: To which is annexed, a number of prayers in other language, upon most occasions. By the Rev Matthew Henry, late of Chester in old England, author of the Exposition of the Old and New Testament* (Wilmington, Del.: James Adams, 1786).

27 This assessment of Dr Archibald Alexander is a very important appreciation of Matthew Henry's *Exposition*, and the full text can readily be accessed on the internet.

When it came to its characteristics, Dr Alexander felt that Matthew Henry had 'a cheerful style', and the reading of it would keep the attention and bring cheer to the soul. He added: 'He must be a very bad man who would become gloomy by the perusal of Henry's Commentary.' He knew that Matthew Henry never lost sight of the fact that the aim of the Scripture was to bring readers to faith, making them wise unto salvation. 'The whole tendency of the work', he asserted, 'is to produce spiritual wisdom, an ardent love of holiness, and a conscientious and diligent regard to all the revealed will of God, in the performance of public and private duties.'

The fact that so many reprints of the *Exposition* occurred in Britain in the nineteenth century is testimony in itself to the value placed on it. Estimates have been made that over 200,000 copies were in circulation by 1850, but no confirmation of this figure is possible. Some information is available to show how well distributed the *Exposition* was in certain areas. For example, for the small county of Kinross in Scotland, A. B. Grosart noted that over a hundred copies of the set were to be found in homes in the county.[28] Also, the inclusion of Matthew Henry in biographical studies along with other nonconformists of the stature of John Howe, Richard Baxter and Samuel Rutherford,[29] or among an even wider group with Tyndale, Hooker, Bunyan and Whitefield,[30] evidence an assessment that his work and character were of the highest order. It is also clear that appreciation of his work was strong among the evangelical Anglicans, probably greater than among the nonconformists, many of whom had deviated from orthodox belief by the middle of the nineteenth century.

A testimony to Matthew Henry's worth as a commentator comes from William Jay (1759-1853). In his autobiography, when he discussed commentators, he wrote:

---

28   A. B. Grosart, *Representative NonConformists*, p. 278.

29   Ibid.

30   See John Stoughton, *Lights of the World*.

But for private and pious use I never found anything comparable to Henry, which, as old John Ryland said, 'a person cannot begin to read without wishing he was shut out from all the world, and able to read it through, without stopping'.[31]

In replying to one of his correspondents he wrote: 'Henry says—it is impossible to read the book of Psalms and not be inflamed or ashamed by the perusal'.[32] Spurgeon was later to point out how indebted William Jay was to Matthew Henry:

> Mr Jay's sermons bear indubitable evidence of his having studied Matthew Henry almost daily. Many of the quaint things in Jay's sermons are either directly traceable to Matthew Henry or to his familiarity with that writer. I have thought that the style of Jay was founded upon Matthew Henry: Matthew Henry is Jay writing, Jay is Matthew Henry preaching. What more could I say in commendation either of the preacher or the author.[33]

Spurgeon himself had an extremely high regard for Matthew Henry, which was shown by his writing the preface to a republication of the *Exposition*. Writing to his own son Charles from Menton in the south of France he gave him this counsel: 'Read Matthew Henry right through, if you can, before you are married; for, after that event, I fear that Jacob may supplant him.'[34] In his *Commenting and Commentaries* he wrote:

> First among the mighty for general usefulness we are bound to mention the man whose name is a household word, Matthew

---

31 *The Autobiography of William Jay* (Edinburgh: Banner of Truth Trust, n.d.), pp. 124-5. The quotation from John Ryland comes from the third edition of his *Contemplations* published in 1777, p. 371.

32 Ibid., p. 235-7. For other testimonies to the influence of Henry's *Exposition*, see Williams, *Memoirs*, pp. 235-7.

33 C. H. Spurgeon, *Commenting and Commentaries: Two Lectures, a catalogue of Bible commentaries and expositions* (Edinburgh: Banner of Truth Trust, 1969), p. 4.

34 *C. H. Spurgeon Autobiography, volume 2: The Full Harvest 1860–1892* (Edinburgh: Banner of Truth Trust, 1973), p. 274.

Henry. He is most pious and pithy, sound and sensible, suggestive and sober, terse and trustworthy. You will find him to be glittering with metaphors, rich in analogies, overflowing with illustrations, superabundant in reflections. He delights in apposition and alliteration; he is usually plain, quaint, and full of pith; he sees right through a text directly; apparently he is not critical, but he quietly gives the result of an accurate critical knowledge of the original fully up to the best critics of his time. He is not versed in the manners and customs of the East, for the Holy Land was not so accessible as in our day; but he is deeply spiritual, heavenly, and profitable; finding good matter in every text, and from all deducing most practical and judicious lessons.[35]

Strong interest from an early period was shown in the Netherlands to Matthew Henry's work, though it took almost fifty years to have all of his *Exposition* translated and published.[36] In 1741 the translation of Genesis appeared from the hand of Reinier Boitet of Delft, and though he expressed the desire to finish the work, that was not to happen. Dirk onder de Linden of Amsterdam took over the responsibilities, and between 1769 and 1787 the New Testament appeared in nineteen parts. The Old Testament was finally completed in 1792.

Between 1909 and 1916, the publishing firm of J. H. Kok, Kampen, brought out a new translation in six volumes, corresponding to the six volumes of the English edition. What is most significant is that the foreword was by the famous theologian, Dr Herman Bavinck (1854-1921) of Kampen. He commended the new translation as being better than the earlier one. Henry was no scholar by calling, Bavinck wrote, and his explanations were lacking in all *display* of scholarship. It was his intention to make people understand the Scripture, not only

---

35 Spurgeon, *Commenting and Commentaries*, p. 2.

36 The best source of information regarding Matthew Henry and his connection with the Netherlands is J. Bout, *Een getuige van het Licht: Het leven van Matthew Henry (1662-1714)* (Houten: Den Hertog B. V., 1994).

as a book that enlightens the past, but also as God's Word that in the present day comes to us and is useful for teaching and correction.[37] Bavinck went on to commend Matthew Henry's exegesis in that he did not seek novel interpretation, but tried to explain the sense of Scripture for Christian believers. He was not surprised that the commentary had been republished so often, or that it had such a place of honour among popular expositions of the Scripture. He concluded his preface with these words:

> [His commentary] is literal and practical, explanatory and applicatory, instructive and comforting. It understands the Scripture as the power of God unto salvation of everyone who believes, as God's Word that abides eternally.

The interest in Matthew Henry increased further in the twentieth century, with numerous reprints of the *Exposition* and the publication of books drawing upon it and also upon his sermons. These include Bible themes from his writings,[38] sermon outlines,[39] devotional books,[40] reprints of particular works,[41] and collections of his writings.[42] However, the greatest impetus to interest in Matthew Henry was probably Dr Leslie

---

37 *Letterlijke en Practicale Verklaring van het Oude Testament door Matthew Henry: Opnieuw uit het Engelsch Vertaald. Vermeerderd met een Voorrede van Dr. H. Bavinck* (Kampen: J. H. Kok, 1912), p. ix.

38 Selwyn Gummer, *Bible Themes from Matthew Henry* (London: Marshall, Morgan & Scott, 1953).

39 Sheldon B. Quincer, ed., *Matthew Henry's Sermon Outlines* (Grand Rapids: Eerdmans, 1955).

40 *Matthew Henry Daily Readings*, ed. Randall Peterson (Fearn: Christian Focus Publications, 2010).

41 *The Young Christian* (Fearn: Christian Focus, 1987); *The Pleasantness of a Religious Life: A Puritan's View of the Good Life* (Fearn: Christian Heritage, 1998); *A Method of Prayer: Freedom in the Face of God* (Fearn: Christian Heritage, 2001).

42 *The Collected Works* (Grand Rapids: Baker Book House, 1979, reprinted 1997); *Family Religion: Principles for raising a godly family* (Fearn: Christian Heritage, 2008).

Church's abridgement of the *Exposition* into a volume of almost 2,000 pages, and 3,000,000 words.[43] He concluded his foreword in this way:

> This one-volume edition we hope will be justified by its usefulness in private devotions, in groups for Bible study, and in the public and private exposition of eternal Truth as revealed in Holy Scripture. This is a valuable aid to the preacher and speaker. It is not a museum-piece, but a sincere and vivid interpretation. It may be that you will not agree with all its conclusions, but it cannot but help you to form your own with confidence.[44]

The benefit of Leslie Church's work is that the actual words of Matthew Henry have been retained, including many of his aphorisms and quaint sayings. This abridgement is still available in several editions, and it has also been translated into Dutch.[45] The fact that modern Christians can still purchase Matthew Henry's *Complete Works* and so many other of his individual works shows that his influence is still being felt, and perhaps at no period since his death has so much of his work been available.

---

43   Leslie F. Church, ed., *Commentary on the Whole Bible by Matthew Henry* (London: Marshall, Morgan and Scott, 1961). Leslie Church was a Methodist who taught at Richmond College (1929–1935), and then served as Connexional Editor for the Methodist Church in Great Britain and Ireland (1935-1953). The last four years of his life were spent on editing this abridgement (1957-1960).

44   Ibid., p. ix.

45   Matthew Henry, *Verklaring van het Oude and het Nieuwe Testament* (Utrecht: Uitgeverij De Banier, 1992).

CONCLUSION

Looking over Matthew Henry's life it is not hard to sum up his main interests. He was dedicated to the Lord Jesus and served him faithfully in his individual life, as a devoted son and brother, as a husband and father, and as a pastor and writer. Early spiritual influences drove him in his Christian commitment and from his allegiance to Christ expressed in his early teenage years he never deviated.

Many things about his life are unknown. Even his full diary is not available for perusal. He kept one, and when his father's diary was published in London in 1884, the editor, Matthew Henry Lee, indicated that shortly 'Matthew Henry's Letters and Diary' would also be published. Clearly this descendant, who published Philip Henry's diary, had access to Matthew's also. That publication never appeared, and there is no way of tracing its present location, assuming it has survived. However, excerpts of the diary appeared in both William Tong's biography and in that by J. B. Williams. Some selections are also given in H. D. Roberts' book, *Matthew Henry and His Chapel 1662-1900*.

From his early days Matthew Henry was a bookworm, so much so that his mother had to try to get him to go out for a walk instead. His diary would appear to be solely given over to his ministerial labours and his own spiritual life. While his father had entries in his diary relating to the farm of Broad Oak, Matthew did not have that same responsibility and hence no corresponding diary entries.

All the references to his family life point to a happy home. He and his wife adopted the children of his sister Ann when she and her husband both died, and they testified to the kindness and love they received from their uncle and aunt. It is clear, though, that Matthew Henry was away from home for a considerable amount of time, as he preached both in areas near to Cheshire and also further afield. Looking back from our perspective he should have had more free time, which would have been good for him and the family, and which also might have given him greater health, especially in the latter part of his life. On one occasion, as we noted previously, he recorded that during his wife's ill-health (she was really in childbirth) he went out in the middle of the night and worked on his commentary in his study. That suggests that work on the commentary brought incessant pressure on him, and he felt obliged to maintain a gruelling schedule of writing. No information exists of how financially rewarding the commentary was to Matthew Henry, but he certainly had money from his parents to study in London and possibly even after being settled in Chester there was a flow of income from his parents. When his new chapel was erected he was the highest donor to the project.

The fact that his commentary has been reprinted so many times testifies to the help that succeeding generations have found in it. The abridgement by Leslie Church has also gone through various printings since its publication in 1960. Not only has the commentary been reprinted, but material has been drawn from it to create new books. This includes those like *Bible Themes from Matthew Henry* and *Sermon Outlines from Matthew Henry*.

Many questions must remain unanswered about Matthew Henry, in spite of him being such a public figure in his day. We have glimpses of him and his relations within and outside his family. We have much of his own writings and no suggestion was ever made by his acquaintances that he was leading a life inconsistent with those expositions. Rather, all references that occur are to his integrity of character and the graces that he displayed. The Christian world has been much more ready to accept and use his literary bequest than to probe into personal details.

I have known and appreciated the writings of Matthew Henry from my teens, and my fuller acquaintance with his works has only strengthened the conviction that he is one of the most significant writers since the Reformation. He never intended to challenge biblical scholarship but rather to utilise all the resources at his disposal for the exposition of Scripture. His writings were intended for the Christian believer, and many of those have had their walk with the Lord strengthened and nourished by them.

What he said shortly before his death, and which is beauti-fully illustrated in all that he did, was 'that a holy, heavenly life, spent in the service of God and communion with him, is the most pleasant and comfortable life that anyone can live in this world'. He truly exhibited these characteristics, and while we may not think his busyness contributed to a comfortable life, yet he certainly felt that his had been a life well spent in the service of God. His life stands as a testimony to God's grace, while his writings continue to enrich the people of God.

GENERAL INDEX

Christian Focus Publications
publishes books for all ages

Our mission statement –

STAYING FAITHFUL
In dependence upon God we seek to impact the world through literature faithful to His infallible Word, the Bible. Our aim is to ensure that the Lord Jesus Christ is presented as the only hope to obtain forgiveness of sin, live a useful life and look forward to heaven with Him.

REACHING OUT
Christ's last command requires us to reach out to our world with His gospel. We seek to help fulfil that by publishing books that point people towards Jesus and help them develop a Christ-like maturity. We aim to equip all levels of readers for life, work, ministry and mission.

Books in our adult range are published in three imprints:

Christian Focus contains popular works including biographies, commentaries, basic doctrine and Christian living. Our children's books are also published in this imprint.

Mentor focuses on books written at a level suitable for Bible College and seminary students, pastors, and other serious readers. The imprint includes commentaries, doctrinal studies, examination of current issues and church history.

Christian Heritage contains classic writings from the past.

Christian Focus Publications Ltd,
Geanies House, Fearn, Ross-shire,
IV20 1TW, Scotland, United Kingdom.
www.christianfocus.com